knitted
animal hats

knitted animal hats

35 wild and wonderful hats and
more for babies, kids, and teens

Fiona Goble

CICO BOOKS
LONDON NEW YORK

Published in 2013 by CICO Books
An imprint of Ryland Peters & Small Ltd
20-21 Jockey's Fields,
London WC1R 4BW
519 Broadway, 5th Floor,
New York, NY 10012

www.cicobooks.com

10 9 8 7 6 5 4 3 2

A CIP catalog record for this book is available from
the Library of Congress and the British Library.

ISBN: 978 1 908862 54 9
Printed in China

Editor: Marie Clayton
Designer: Barbara Zuñiga
Pattern checker: Tricia McKenzie
Photographers: Terry Benson, Penny Wincer,
Emma Mitchell
Stylists: Rob Merrett, Clare Hunt
Illustrators: Stephen Dew, Kate Simunek

For digital editions, visit
www.cicobooks.com/aps.php

contents

Introduction   6

CHAPTER 1
Tiny Hats for Teeny Babies 8

Squawk the Chick	10
Spot the Ladybug	12
Spot the Ladybug bootees	15
Rudy the Rabbit	16
Tweet the Robin	18
Buzzy Bee	20
Buzzy Bee bootees	22

CHAPTER 2
Cozy Hats for Cute Kids 24

Hoot the Owl	26
Ribbit the Frog	29
Prickle the Hedgehog	31
Savannah the Zebra	34
Savannah the Zebra wrist warmers	37
Boo the Monster	38
Squeak the Mouse	40
Rumble Bear	42
Rumble Bear mittens	45
Otto the Octopus	46
Waddle the Penguin	48
Nana the Monkey	50
Gurgle the Fish	52
Leandro the Lion	54
Rusty the Fox	58
Blizzard the Reindeer	62
Scorch the Dragon	65
Bamboo the Panda	68

CHAPTER 3
Cool Hats for the Young at Heart 70

Ozzie the Koala	72
Slinky Cat	74
Slinky Cat mittens	77
Kitty the Tiger	78
Kitty the Tiger boot toppers	80
Hunter the Hound	81
Pattie the Cow	84
Pattie the Cow ankle warmers	87
Curly the Pig	88
Frosty the Polar Bear	90

CHAPTER 4
Useful Information 92

Tools & Materials	94
Stitches & Techniques	95
Yarn Information	108
Suppliers	110
Index	111
Acknowledgments	112

introduction

If you love knitting, have a penchant for fancy hats, and adore animals, then I hope this will be just the book you're after! I loved the craze for wacky animal headgear and wanted to help people create their own one-of-a-kind hats quickly and easily. Some of the hat patterns are suitable for new knitters and would make an ideal second or third knitting project. Others are more suitable for knitters with a few projects already under their belt—and a few are aimed at knitters with a bit more experience. The skill level required for each project is clearly marked on the patterns themselves. If you haven't picked up your needles for a while and want to brush up your skills, have a look through the Useful Information section on pages 92-107.

The patterns are divided into three sections: hats for babies; hats for younger kids; and hats for the "young at heart"—that's pretty much everyone from pre-teens upward who fancies sporting an animal hat! Have a leaf through and see which styles you like best—and don't forget that most of the patterns in Cozy Hats for Cute Kids (pages 24-69) and Cool Hats for the Young at Heart (pages 70-91) include instructions for two sizes, so you can knit the smaller version for young kids and the bigger version for older kids, teens, and adults.

In case you haven't already spotted them, as well as the hats there are a few must-have accessories. For little babies, there are gorgeous bootees to match the ladybug and bee hats. And if you're a little older, check out the zebra-striped wrist warmers, cow ankle warmers, and tiger-striped boot toppers.

All the projects are knitted in standard yarns. If you can't find the yarn specified, or just fancy something a bit different, you can substitute a similar yarn of the same thickness—see the Yarn Information on pages 108-109. Just remember to knit your gauge (tension) square first, so you can be sure that your finished creation will be the right size.

The wonderful thing about knitting is how little equipment you need. To make sure that you have everything, take a look at page 94 and also check out the information given in the individual patterns. I've absolutely adored creating these hats and seeing my "menagerie" come together from the balls of yarn in my knitting basket—and I hope that you will have just as much fun recreating and wearing them.

Chapter 1

tiny hats
for teeny babies

squawk the chick 10

spot the ladybug 12

spot the ladybug bootees 15

rudy the rabbit 16

tweet the robin 18

buzzy bee 20

buzzy bee bootees 22

squawk the chick

What self-respecting baby could do without this warm and fuzzy, charming chick beanie to ward off the chilly breezes in cooler climes? The hat is knitted in a chunky-weight yellow yarn, but if you fancy a tiny knitted blackbird or a blue oriole—just choose yarn accordingly. The hat is super-quick to knit and an ideal project for beginners.

Yarn
1 x 1¾ oz (50 g) ball—approx 81 yds (75 m)—Sirdar Click Chunky in shade 186 Lemon (A)
Small amount of Sirdar Country Style DK in shade 412 White (B) and shade 473 Slate (C)
Small amount of Rowan Wool Cotton DK in shade 985 Cafe (D)

You will also need
Sizes US 9 (5.5 mm) and US 3 (3.25 mm) knitting needles
Yarn sewing needle
Large-eyed embroidery needle

Sizes
0-6 months (6-12 months)

Actual measurements
Approx 13½ in/34 cm (15 in/38 cm) circumference

Gauge (tension)
16 sts and 22 rows to 4 in (10 cm) square over stockinette (stocking) stitch using US 9 (5.5 mm) needles.

Main hat
(*make 1*)
Using US 9 (5.5 mm) needles and A, cast on 54(60) sts.
Row 1: [K1, p1] to end.
Row 2: [P1, k1] to end.
Rep Rows 1-2 once more.
Work 18(20) rows in st st beg with a k row.
Large size only:
Next row: K4, [k2tog, k8] 5 times, k2tog, k4. (54 sts)
Next row: P.
Both sizes:
Next row: K3, [sl1, k2tog, psso, k6] 5 times, sl1, k2tog, psso, k3. (42 sts)
Next and every WS row until stated otherwise: P.
Next RS row: K2, [sl1, k2tog, psso, k4] 5 times, sl1, k2tog, psso, k2. (30 sts)
Next RS row: K1, [sl1, k2tog, psso, k2] 5 times, sl1, k2tog, psso, k1. (18 sts)
Next row (WS): [P2tog] to end. (9 sts)
Next row: [Sl1, k2tog, psso] 3 times. (3 sts)
Work 7 rows in st st beg with a p row.
Bind (cast) off.

Outer eyes
(*make 2*)
Using US 3 (3.25 mm) needles and B, cast on 5 sts.
Row 1: Inc1, k to last 2 sts, inc1, k1. (7 sts)
Row 2: P.
Rep first 2 rows 3 times more. (13 sts)
Row 9: K1, k2tog, k to last 3 sts, ssk, k1. (11 sts)
Row 10: P.
Rep Rows 9-10 twice more. (7 sts)
Row 15: K1, K2tog, k3, ssk, k1. (5 sts)
Bind (cast) off.

Beak
Using US 3 (3.25 mm) needles and D, cast on 8 sts.
Work 2 rows in st st beg with a k row.
Row 3: K2tog, k to last 2 sts, ssk. (6 sts)
Row 4: P.
Rep Rows 3-4 once more. (4 sts)
Row 7: K2tog, ssk. (2 sts)
Row 8: P2tog. (1 st)
Break yarn and pull through rem st.

Making up and finishing

For general information on putting your hat together, see pages 104–107.

With RS of hat facing outward, oversew seam of "stalk" at top of hat. Join back seam of hat using the flat-seam technique (see page 104).

Oversew eyes in place. Using C, embroider a coil of chain stitch (see page 106) for each eye center.

Oversew beak in place.

spot the ladybug

With their bright, red-spotted backs, ladybugs (ladybirds) are one of the show stealers of the insect world. Grab a slice of the action by knitting this cheerful hat to add a splash of scarlet to a dull day. It's knitted in soft DK yarn and, as the spots are embroidered on afterward, it's much easier to knit than it looks. Don't forget to check out the ladybug bootees on page 15 to complete the look!

Yarn
1 x 1¾ oz (50 g) ball—approx 127 yds (116 m)—Debbie Bliss Rialto DK in shade 12 Red (A)
1 x 1¾ oz (50 g) ball—approx 127 yds (116 m)—Sublime Extra Fine Merino in shade 13 Jet Black (B)
Small amount of Patons Diploma Gold DK in shade 6184 Steel (C)

You will also need
Size US 5 (3.75 mm) knitting needles
Yarn sewing needle
Large-eyed embroidery needle

Sizes
0-6 months (6-12 months)

Actual measurements
Approx 12 in/30 cm (13¾ in/35 cm) circumference

Gauge (tension)
24 sts and 30 rows to 4 in (10 cm) square over stockinette (stocking) stitch using US 5 (3.75 mm) needles.

Notes
Before you begin knitting, prepare a small ball of A consisting of 9 yds (8 m) of yarn.

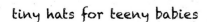

Hat
(*make 1*)
Using US 5 (3.75 mm) needles and main ball of A, cast on 72(84) sts.
K 6 rows.
Leave A at side of work and join in B.
K 2 rows. Break B.
Row 9: K30(36) in A, rejoin B, k12 in B, join in small ball of A, k30(36) in A.
Row 10: P30(36) in A, p12 in B, p30(36) in A.
Work 2 more rows in st st beg with a k row and keeping to A/B patt as set.
Row 13: K31(37) in A, k10 in B, k31(37) in A.
Row 14: P32(38) in A, p8 in B, p32(38) in A.
Row 15: K33(39) in A, k6 in B, k33(39) in A.
Row 16: P34(40) in A, p4 in B, p34(40) in A.
Break A toward center of work.
Using A, work 4 rows in st st beg with a k row.
Row 21: K35(41) in A, k2 in B, k35(41) in A.
Row 22: P35(41) in A, p2 in B, p35(41) in A.
Rep Rows 21-22 eight times more.
Large size only:
Row 39: Using A, k6, [k2tog, k12] twice, k2tog, k5; using B, k2; using A, k5, [ssk, k12] twice, ssk, k6. (78 sts)
Row 40: P38 in A, p2 in B, p38 in A.
Row 41: Using A, k5, [sl1, k2tog, psso, k10] twice, sl1, k2tog, psso, k4; using B, k2; using A, k4, [sl1, k2tog, psso, k10] twice, sl1, k2tog, psso, k5. (66 sts)
Small size only:
Row 39: Using A, k5, [k2tog, k10] twice, k2tog, k4; using B, k2; using A, k4, [ssk, k10] twice, ssk, k5. (66 sts)
Both sizes:
Next row: P32 in A, p2 in B, p32 in A.
Next row: Using A, k4, [sl1, k2tog, psso, k8] twice, sl1, k2tog, psso, k3; using B, k2; using A, k3, [sl1, k2tog, psso, k8] twice, sl1, k2tog, psso, k4. (54 sts)
Next row: P26 in A, p2 in B, p26 in A.
Next row: Using A, k3, [sl1, k2tog, psso, k6] twice, sl1, k2tog, psso, k2; using B, k2; using A, k2, [sl1, k2tog, psso, k6] twice, sl1, k2tog, psso, k3. (42 sts)
Next row: P20 in A, p2 in B, p20 in A.
Next row: Using A, k2, [sl1, k2tog, psso, k4] twice, sl1, k2tog, psso, k1; using B, k2; using A, k1, [sl1, k2tog, psso, k4] twice, sl1, k2tog, psso, k2. (30 sts)

Next row: P14 in A, p2 in B, p14 in A.
Next row: Using A, k1, [sl1, k2tog, psso, k2] twice, sl1, k2tog, psso; using B, k2; using A, [sl1, k2tog, psso, k2] twice, sl1, k2tog, psso, k1. (18 sts)
Next row: Using A, [p2tog] 4 times; using B, p2tog; using A, [p2tog] 4 times. (9 sts)
Next row: Using A, [sl1, k2tog, psso] 3 times. (3 sts)
Break yarn leaving a long tail.
Thread yarn tail through rem sts, pull up tightly and secure.

Making up and finishing
For general information on putting your hat together, see pages 104–107.
Join back seam of hat using the flat-seam technique (see page 104).

Using B, embroider six small coils of chain stitch (see page 106) for spots.

Using B, embroider a row of chain stitch round sides and top of ladybug's head. Using B, work antennae in stem stitch (see page 106).

Using C, embroider a small ring of chain stitch for each eye. Using B, work a French knot (see page 106) in center of each eye.

Using C, embroider mouth in chain stitch.

spot the ladybug bootees

What style-conscious mother could resist these ultra-cute ladybug (ladybird) bootees, designed for a baby's winter wardrobe? Knitted in soft scarlet and black yarns, these are the perfect accessory to keep delicate little feet extra toasty when the temperature dips. Don't forget to add the matching hat on page 12.

Bootee
(*make 2*)

Using US 3 (3.25 mm) needles and A, cast on 34(38) sts.
Row 1: [K2, p2] to last 2 sts, k2.
Row 2: [P2, k2] to last 2 sts, p2.
Rep last 2 rows 5(6) times more.
Break yarn.
Put first 10(11) sts on the first pin or stitch holder. Rejoin A, k14(16). Put rem 10(11) sts on second pin or stitch holder.
Cont working 14(16) sts on needle only.
Work 13(15) rows in st st beg with a p row.
Break A and join in B.
Large size only:
Row 31: K1, k2tog, k10, ssk, k1. (14sts)
Row 32: K.
Row 33: K1, k2tog, k8, ssk, k1. (12 sts)
Row 34: P.
Small size only:
Row 27: K1, k2tog, k8, ssk, k1. (12 sts)
Row 28: K.
Both sizes:
Next row: K1, k2tog, k6, ssk, k1. (10 sts)
Next row: P.
Next row: K1, k2tog, k4, ssk, k1. (8 sts)
Next row: P2tog, p4, p2tog. (6 sts)
Break yarn and leave last 6 sts (which will form the toe end) on needle.
Starting at heel edge of cuff and with RS facing, k10(11) sts from first stitch holder (you may find it easier to transfer them to a spare needle first), pick up 11(13) sts evenly up side of foot part of bootee, k6 sts from needle, pick up 11(13) sts evenly down second side, k10(11) sts from second stitch holder. (48/54 sts)
K 7 rows.
Shape sole:
Next row: K.
Next row: P.
Large size only:
Next row: K2tog, k to last 2 sts, ssk. (52 sts)
Next row: P2tog, p22, [p2tog] twice, p22, p2tog. (48 sts)
Both sizes:
Next row: K2tog, k20, ssk, k2tog, k20, ssk. (44 sts)

Yarn
1 x 1¾ oz (50 g) ball–approx 127 yds (116 m)–
Debbie Bliss Rialto DK in shade 12 Red (A)
1 x 1¾ oz (50 g) ball–approx 127 yds (116 m)–
Sublime Extra Fine Merino in shade 13 Jet
Black (B)

You will also need
Size US 3 (3.25 mm) knitting needles
Yarn sewing needle
2 large safety pins or stitch holders

Sizes
0-6 months (6-12 months)

Actual measurements
Approx 3¾ in/9.5 cm (4¼ in/11 cm) length of sole

Gauge (tension)
26 sts and 40 rows to 4 in (10 cm) square over stockinette (stocking) stitch using US 3 (3.25 mm) needles.

Next row: P2tog, p18, [p2tog] twice, p18, p2tog. (40 sts)
Next row: K2tog, k16, ssk, k2tog, k16, ssk. (36 sts)
Next row: P2tog, p14, [p2tog] twice, p14, p2tog. (32 sts)
Bind (cast) off.

Making up and finishing
Using B, join heel seams using the flat-seam technique (see page 104). Using A, join ribbed section at back of each bootee.

With RS of bootee together, oversew sole seam. Using B, work a line of chain stitch (see page 106) up center top of each bootee. Using B, work four French knots (see page 106) for spots.

rudy the rabbit

You'd need a heart of steel to say "no" to a toddler dressed in this classy bunny bonnet. Knitted in a pretty shade of dusky pink, the basic hat is made from a simple rectangle, seamed together to form a pixie-like hood. If you've mastered the art of picking up stitches along a knitted edge, you'll find this impressive hat easy to knit. Choose pink or baby blue—or knit it in the colors of a real-life rabbit you know.

Yarn
1 x 1¾ oz (50 g) ball—approx 127 yds (116 m)—
   Wendy Merino DK in shade 2370 Fuchsia
¾ in (17 mm) dusky pink button
Sewing thread to match knitting yarn

You will also need
Size US 5 (3.75 mm) knitting needles
Yarn sewing needle
Standard sewing needle

Sizes
One size to fit 6-12 months

Actual measurements
Approx 11 in/28 cm neck circumference,
   7½ in/19 cm height

Gauge (tension)
23 sts and 30 rows to 4 in
   (10 cm) square over
   stockinette (stocking) stitch
   using US 5 (3.75 mm) needles.

Main hat
(*make 1*)
Using US 5 (3.75 mm) needles, cast on 78 sts.
Row 1: [K2, p2] to last 2 sts, k2.
Row 2: [P2, k2] to last 2 sts, p2.
Rep Rows 1-2 twice more.
Row 7: [K2, p2] to last 2 sts, k2.
Work 41 rows in st st beg with a p row.
Bind (cast) off.

With RS of work facing, pick up and k 27 sts down one side of hat, beg at ribbed section, then pick up and k 27 sts down other side of hat, beginning at bound- (cast-) off edge.
(54 sts)
Turn work and cast on 16 sts. (70 sts)
Next row: [K2, p2] to last 2 sts, k2.
Next row: [P2, k2] to last 2 sts, p2.
Next row: [K2, p2] to last 2 sts, k2.
Next row: [P2, k2] to last 6 sts, bind (cast) off 2 sts kwise (for buttonhole), k1, p2. (68 sts)
Next row: K2, p2, turn work and cast on 2 sts, turn work again, [p2, k2] to end. (70 sts)
Next row: [P2, k2] to last 2 sts, p2.
Next row: [K2, p2] to last 2 sts, k2.
Bind (cast) off loosely, keeping to p2, k2 patt as set until last 16 sts.
Bind (cast) off these last 16 sts pwise.

Ears
(*make 4 pieces*)
Using US 5 (3.75 mm) needles, cast on 7 sts.
Work 26 rows in st st beg with a k row.
Row 27: K1, k2tog, k1, ssk, k1. (5 sts)
Row 28: P2tog, p1, p2tog. (3 sts)
Row 29: Sl1, k2tog, psso. (1 st)
Break yarn and pull through rem st.

Making up and finishing
For general information on putting your hat together, see pages 104-107.

Join back seam of hat using mattress stitch (see page 104).

Place two ear pieces RS together and oversew (see page 105) round sides and top, leaving lower edge open for turning. Turn ear RS out and oversew lower edge. Make second ear in the same way. Stitch ears in place.

Sew button in place.

tweet the robin

When you're away from the warmth of your nest, there's no better way to keep warm than to keep your head tucked into your very own robin redbreast hat. Knitted in the softest of fawn yarns, this hat is a great first project for anyone just starting out on mixing colors in their knitting and would make an ideal gift for a newborn baby girl or boy.

Yarn
1 x 3½ oz (100 g) ball–approx 262 yds (240 m)– Katia Merino Blend DK in shade 37 Umber (A)
1 x 1¾ oz (50 g) ball–approx 127 yds (116 m)–Rowan Amy Butler Belle Organic DK in shade 020 Clementine (B)
Small amount of Katia Merino Blend DK in shade 19 Gold (C)
Small amount of Sirdar Country Style DK in shade 417 Black (D)

You will also need
Sizes US 5 (3.75 mm) and US 3 (3.25 mm) knitting needles
Yarn sewing needle
Large-eyed embroidery needle
Size D-3 (3.25 mm) crochet hook

Sizes
0-6 months (6-12 months)

Actual measurements
Approx 13 in/33 cm (15 in/38 cm) circumference

Gauge (tension)
22 sts and 30 rows to 4 in (10 cm) square over stockinette (stocking) stitch using US 5 (3.75 mm) needles.

Notes
Before you begin knitting, prepare a separate ball of A consisting of 8 yds (7.5 m) of yarn.

Hat
(*make 1*)
Using US 5 (3.75 mm) needles, cast on 23(29) sts in separate ball of A, 26 sts in B, and 23(29) sts in A from main ball. (72/84 sts)
Place a small safety pin marker at 23rd(29th) st in from each edge.
K 4 rows keeping to A/B patt as set.
Work 4 rows in st st beg with a k row and keeping to A/B patt as set.
Row 9: K24(30) in A, k24 in B, k24(30) in A.
Row 10: P25(31) in A, p22 in B, p25(31) in A.
Row 11: K26(32) in A, k20 in B, k26(32) in A.
Row 12: P27(33) in A, p18 in B, p27(33) in A.
Row 13: K28(34) in A, k16 in B, k28(34) in A.
Row 14: P29(35) in A, p14 in B, p29(35) in A.
Cont in A only, break all yarns no longer in use.
K 2 rows.
Work 18 rows in st st beg with a k row.
Large size only:
Row 35: K6, [k2tog, k12] 3 times, [ssk, k12] twice, ssk, k6. (78 sts)
Row 36: P.
Row 37: K5, [sl1, k2tog, psso, k10] 5 times, sl1, k2tog, psso, k5. (66 sts)
Small size only:
Row 35: K5, [k2tog, k10] 3 times, [ssk, k10] twice, ssk, k5. (66 sts)
Both sizes:
Next and every WS row: P.
Next RS row: K4, [sl1, k2tog, psso, k8] 5 times, sl1, k2tog, psso, k4. (54 sts)
Next RS row: K3, [sl1, k2tog, psso, k6] 5 times, sl1, k2tog, psso, k3. (42 sts)
Next RS row: K2, [sl1, k2tog, psso, k4] 5 times, sl1, k2tog, psso, k2. (30 sts)
Next RS row: K1, [sl1, k2tog, psso, k2] 5 times, sl1, k2tog, psso, k1. (18 sts)
Next RS row: [P2tog] to end. (9 sts)
Next row: [sl1, k2tog, psso] 3 times. (3 sts)
Work 7 rows in st st beg with a p row.
Bind (cast) off.

With RS of work facing and using A, pick up and k 23(29) sts across lower edge from RH edge toward first safety pin marker.
K 4 rows.
Next row: K2tog, k to end. (22/28 sts)
Next row: K to last 2 sts, ssk. (21/27 sts)
Rep last 2 rows once more. (20/26 sts)
Next row: K2tog, k to end. (19/25 sts)
Bind (cast) off.

With RS of work facing and using A, pick up and k 23(29) sts across lower edge from second safety pin marker to LH edge.
K 4 rows.
Next row: K to last 2 sts, ssk. (22/28 sts)
Next row: K2tog, k to end. (21/27 sts)
Rep last 2 rows once more. (20/26 sts)
Next row: K to last 2 sts, ssk. (19/25 sts)
Bind (cast) off.

Beak
Using US 3 (3.25 mm) needles and C, cast on 8 sts.
Row 1: K2tog, k4, ssk. (6 sts)
Row 2 and every WS row until stated otherwise: P.
Row 3 (RS): K2tog, k2, ssk. (4 sts)
Row 5 (RS): K2tog, ssk. (2 sts)
Row 6 (WS): P2tog. (1 st)
Break yarn and pull through rem st.

Making up and finishing
For general information on putting your hat together, see pages 104–107.

With RS of hat facing, oversew seam of "stalk." Join back seam using the flat-seam technique (see page 104).

Using tails at lower edge of hat, work a crochet edging (see page 107) just up short inside edges of lower part of hat.

Using D, work a small coil of chain stitch (see page 106) for each eye. Using a separated strand of D, work three straight stitches above each eye for eyelashes.

Oversew beak in place.

buzzy bee

Turn the baby in your life into a friendly bumblebee in this endearing yellow-and-black striped headgear. With its roll-up brim, wear it pulled well down to keep the wind out on cool days. Or roll up the brim a little for a jaunty look when the weather is slightly more clement. And to complete that bumblebee look, why not knit the matching baby bootees on page 22?

Yarn
1 x 1¾ oz (50 g) ball–approx 127 yds (116 m)–
    of Sublime Extra Fine Merino in shade 13
    Jet Black (A)
1 x 3½ oz (100 g) ball–approx 262 yds (240 m)–
    of Katia Merino Blend in shade 19 Gold (B)
Small amounts of Sirdar Country Style DK in
    shade 411 Cream (C) and shade 473 Slate (D)

You will also need
Size US 5 (3.75 mm) knitting needles
Yarn sewing needle
Large-eyed embroidery needle

Sizes
0-6 months (6-12 months)

Actual measurements
Approx 12 in/30 cm
    (13¾ in/35 cm)
    circumference

Gauge (tension)
24 sts and 28 rows to
    4 in (10 cm) square over
    stockinette (stocking)
    stitch using US 5
    (3.75 mm) needles.

Hat
(*make 1*)
Using US 5 (3.75 mm) needles and A, cast on 72(84) sts.
Work 8(10) rows in st st beg with a k row.
Join in B.
Next row: K30(36) in B, k12 in A, k30(36) in B.
Next row: P30(36) in B, p12 in A, p30(36) in B.
Rep last 2 rows once more.
Using A, work 4 rows in st st, beg with a k row.
Next row: K32(38) in B, k8 in A, k32(38) in B.
Next row: P33(39) in B, p6 in A, p33(39) in B.
Using B, work 2 rows in st st, beg with a k row.
Using A, work 4 rows in st st, beg with a k row.
Using B, work 4 rows in st st, beg with a k row.
For a longer hat, rep last 8 rows once more to add
2 extra stripes.
Large size only:
Using A, work 2 rows in st st, beg with a k row.
Next row: K6, [k2tog, k12] 3 times,
[ssk, k12] twice, ssk, k6. (78 sts)
Next row: P.
Next row: Using B, k5, [sl1, k2tog,
psso, k10] 5 times, sl1, k2tog, psso,
k5. (66 sts)
Small size only:
Using A, work 4 rows in st st, beg
with a k row.
Next row: Using B, k5, [k2tog, k10]
3 times, [ssk, k10] twice, ssk, k5.
(66 sts)
Both sizes:
Next and every WS row: P, using
same yarn color as previous row
worked.
Next RS row: Using B, k4, [sl1,
k2tog, psso, k8] 5 times, sl1,
k2tog, psso, k4. (54 sts)
Next RS row: Using A, k3, [sl1,
k2tog, pkso, k6] 5 times, sl1,
k2tog, pkso, k3. (42 sts)
Next RS row: Using A, k2, [sl1,
k2tog, psso, k4] 5 times, sl1,
k2tog, psso, k2. (30 sts)
Next RS row: Using B, k1, [sl1,
k2tog, pkso, k2] 5 times, sl1,
k2tog, pkso, k1. (18 sts)

Next RS row: Using B, [k2tog] 9 times. (9 sts)
Next RS row: Using A, [k2tog] twice, k1, [k2tog] twice.
(5 sts)
Using A, work 9 rows in st st beg with a p row.
Bind (cast) off.

Making up and finishing
For general information on putting your hat together, see pages 104–107.

With RS of hat facing outward, oversew seam of "stalk" at top of hat using A. Using same yarn, join back seam of hat using the flat-seam technique (see page 104).

Using C, work a small circle of chain stitch (see page 106) for each eye. Using A, work a French knot (see page 106) at center of each eye.

Using D, embroider antenna in chain stitch.

The hat can be made to fit snugly, as in the version left, or a little longer, as shown on the baby. To make the longer hat, you will need to add an extra stripe in each of black (A) and yellow (B) where indicated in the pattern.

buzzy bee bootees

These soft black and yellow striped bee bootees with their mohair wings are the ideal footwear to keep tiny toes warm on cooler days. With their ribbed tops, you can be sure that the bootees will stay on small feet. And while you've got your needles out, don't forget to accessorize the bootees with the charming little bumblebee hat on page 20.

Yarn
1 x 1¾ oz (50 g) ball—approx 127 yds (116 m)—of
    Sublime Extra Fine Merino in shade 13 Jet Black (A)
1 x 3½ oz (100 g) ball—approx 262 yds (240 m)—of
    Katia Merino Blend in shade 19 Gold (B)
Small amount of Debbie Bliss Angel in shade 1 White (C)

You will also need
Sizes US 3 (3.25 mm) and US 5 (3.75 mm) knitting
    needles
Yarn sewing needle
2 large safety pins or stitch holders

Sizes
0-6 months (6-12 months)

Actual measurements
Approx 3¾ in/9.5 cm (4¼ in/11 cm) length of sole

Gauge (tension)
26 sts and 40 rows to 4 in (10 cm) square over
    stockinette (stocking) stitch using US 3
    (3.25 mm) needles.

Bootee
(*make 2*)
Using US 3 (3.25 mm) needles and A, cast on 34(38) sts.
Row 1: [K2, p2] to last 2 sts, k2.
Row 2: [P2, k2] to last 2 sts, p2.
Rep last 2 rows 11(13) times more.
Break yarn.
Put first 10(11) sts on the first pin or stitch holder. Join B, k14(16). Put remaining 10(11) sts on the second pin or stitch holder.
Cont on 14(16) sts on needle only.
Next row: Using B, p.
Using A, work 2 rows in st st beg with a k row.
Rep last 4 rows 2(3) times more, keeping to the 2 rows B, 2 rows A pattern.
Using B, work 2 rows in st st beg with a k row.
Break B and knit rem bootee in A only.
Next row: K1, k2tog, k8(10), ssk, k1. (12/14 sts)
Next row: K.
Next row: K1, k2tog, k6(8), ssk, k1. (10/12 sts)
Large size only:
Next row: P2tog, p8, p2tog. (10 sts)
Next row: K.
Both sizes:
Next row: P.
Next row: K1, k2tog, k4, ssk, k1. (8 sts)
Next row: P2tog, p4, p2tog. (6 sts)
Break yarn and leave these 6 sts (which will form the toe end) on the needle.
Starting at heel edge of cuff and with RS facing, k10(11) sts from first stitch holder (you may find it easier to transfer them to a spare needle first), pick up 11(13) sts evenly up side of foot part of bootee, k6 sts from needle, pick up 11(13) sts evenly down second side, then k10(11) sts from second stitch holder.
(48/54 sts)
K 7 rows.

Shape sole:
Next row: K.
Next row: P.
Large size only:
Next row: K2tog, k to last 2 sts, ssk. (52 sts)
Next row: P2tog, p22, [p2tog] twice, p22, p2tog. (48 sts)
Both sizes:
Next row: K2tog, k20, ssk, k2tog, k20, ssk. (44 sts)
Next row: P2tog, p18, [p2tog] twice, p18, p2tog. (40 sts)
Next row: K2tog, k16, ssk, k2tog, k16, ssk. (36 sts)
Next row: P2tog, p14, [p2tog] twice, p14, p2tog. (32 sts)
Bind (cast) off.

Wings
(*make 2*)
Using US 5 (3.75 mm) needles and C, cast on 4 sts.
Row 1: [Inc1, k1] twice. (6 sts)
Row 2: P.

Row 3: Inc1, k3, inc1, k1. (8 sts)
Work 11 rows in st st beg with a k row.
Row 15: K2tog, k4, ssk. (6 sts)
Row 16: P.
Row 17: K2tog, k2, ssk. (4 sts)
Bind (cast) off kwise on WS.

Making up and finishing
Using A, join back and heel seams using the flat-seam technique (see page 104).

With RS of bootee together, oversew sole seam. Thread yarn tails on wing pieces down sides to center. Use yarn tails to secure wings to top of bootees.

Chapter 2

cozy hats
for cute kids

hoot the owl 26

ribbit the frog 29

prickle the hedgehog 31

savannah the zebra 34

savannah the zebra wrist warmers 37

boo the monster 38

squeak the mouse 40

rumble bear 42

rumble bear mittens 45

otto the octopus 46

waddle the penguin 48

nana the monkey 50

gurgle the fish 52

leandro the lion 54

rusty the fox 58

blizzard the reindeer 62

scorch the dragon 65

bamboo the panda 68

hoot the owl

With wings to keep little ones' ears extra warm, this adorable owl will look perfect perched on the head of any fashion-conscious child. It is knitted in a chunky tweed yarn that looks just like an owl's flecked feathers. And its eye fringe is cunningly knitted using a special version of garter stitch. You can knit your owl hat in a colorful combination of yarns as shown here—or choose rustic, natural tones for a more realistic looking creature.

Yarn
1(2) x 1¾ oz (50 g) ball(s)—each approx 81 yds (75 m)—Sirdar Connemara Chunky in shade 352 Homestead (A)
Small amounts of Sirdar Country Style DK in shade 411 Cream (B), shade 527 Rosehip (C), and shade 417 Black (D)
Small amount of Debbie Bliss Rialto DK in shade 44 Aqua (E)
Small amount of Wendy Merino DK in shade 2370 Fuchsia (F)

You will also need
Sizes US 9 (5.5 mm) and US 3 (3.25) knitting needles
Size US 7 (4.5 mm) or similar size crochet hook
Yarn sewing needle
Large-eyed embroidery needle

Sizes
3–10 years (11 years and over)

Actual measurements
Approx 15½ in/40 cm (19 in/48 cm) circumference

Gauge (tension)
16 sts and 22 rows to 4 in (10 cm) square over stockinette (stocking) stitch using US 9 (5.5 mm) needles.

Main hat
(*make 1*)
Using US 9 (5.5 mm) needles and A, cast on 64(76) sts.
Work 30(34) rows in st st beg with a k row.
Bind (cast) off.

Earflaps
(*make 2*)
With RS facing and using US 9 (5.5 mm) needles and A, pick up and k 12(14)sts along cast-on edge for first earflap.
Work 3 rows in st st beg with a p row.
Large size only:
Row 3: K1, k2tog, k to last 3 sts, ssk, k1. (12 sts)
Work 3 rows in st st beg with a p row.
Both sizes:
Next row: K1, k2tog, k to last 3 sts, ssk, k1. (10 sts)
Work 3 rows in st st beg with a p row.
Rep last 4 rows once more. (8 sts)
Next row: K1, k2tog, k2, ssk, k1. (6 sts)
Next row: P.
Next row: K1, k2tog, ssk, k1. (4 sts)
Next row: [P2tog] twice. (2 sts)
Next row: K2tog. (1 st)
Break yarn and pull through rem st.
Work second earflap in the same way.

Tassel owl ears
Cut twelve 2¾ in (7 cm) lengths of A, plus two 8 in (20 cm) lengths of A for tying and fastening tassels.

> **Tip**
> Before picking up stitches for the earflaps, fold the main hat piece together, so the two short ends meet at the center. Place a small safety pin at each side of the hat at the cast-on edge to mark the center of each earflap. Pick up an equal number of stitches on either side of the marker for each earflap.

Arrange shorter lengths of yarn into two bunches of six and tie securely at centers using longer yarn lengths.

Outer eyes
(*make 2*)
Using US 3 (3.25 mm) needles and B, cast on 5 sts.
Row 1: Inc1, k to last 2 sts, inc1, k1. (7 sts)
Row 2: P.
Rep Rows 1–2 three times more. (13 sts)
Row 9: K1, k2tog, k to last 3 sts, ssk, k1. (11 sts)
Row 10: P.
Rep Rows 9–10 twice more. (7 sts)
Row 15: K1, k2tog, k1, ssk, k1. (5 sts)
Bind (cast) off kwise on WS of work.

Eye fringes
(*make 2*)
The fringes are knitted in extended garter stitch (see page 98).
Using US 3 (3.25 mm) needles and E, cast on 28 sts.
Row 1: K.
Row 2: K, but wind yarn 3 times round needle for each st instead of only once.
Row 3: K.
Bind (cast) off.

Beak
(*make 1*)
Using US 3 (3.25 mm) needles and C, cast on 10 sts.
Work 2 rows in st st beg with a k row.
Row 3: K2tog, k to last 2 sts, ssk. (8 sts)
Row 4: P.

Rep Rows 3–4 twice more. (4 sts)
Row 9: K2tog, ssk. (2 sts)
Row 10: P2tog. (1 st)
Break yarn and pull through rem st.

Making up and finishing
For general information on putting your hat together, see pages 104–107.

Join back seam of hat using the flat-seam technique and top of hat using mattress stitch (see page 104).

Stitch owl ear tassels in place using ends of yarn secured round center of tassels. Trim tassels to about 2³/₄ in (7 cm) and separate yarn strands using tip of needle used to sew hat together.

Oversew beak and outer eyes in place. Using D, embroider a coil of chain stitch (see page 106) for each eye center. Fold eye fringes in half lengthwise and oversew cast-on and bound- (cast-) off edges. Oversew edge in place around eyes.

Using the crochet hook and a doubled strand of F, work a crochet edging (see page 107) around entire lower edge of hat, beginning and ending at back seam.

ribbit the frog

This particular frog is beautifully warm and soft, not cold and slimy–thankfully–like his real-life relations. With goggle-eyes and on the lookout for some unsuspecting fly to snack on, the frog hat is knitted in a smooth yarn in a subtle shade of lime green. But if your taste is a little more tropical, try knitting him in bright blue or deep crimson.

Yarn
2 x 1¾ oz (50 g) balls–each approx 98 yds (90 m)–
    Patons Fairytale Dreamtime DK in shade 4952
    Lime (A)
Small amounts of Sirdar Country Style DK in shade
    473 Slate (B) and shade 412 White (C)
Small amount of fiberfill toy stuffing

You will also need
Sizes US 5 (3.75 mm) and US 3 (3.25 mm) knitting
    needles
Size US D-3 (3.25 mm) crochet hook
Yarn sewing needle
Large-eyed embroidery needle
2 small safety pins

Sizes
To fit 1-3 (4-5) years

Actual measurements
Approx 14½ in/37 cm (15½ in/39 cm) circumference

Gauge (tension)
23 sts and 30 rows to 4 in (10
cm) square over stockinette
(stocking) stitch using
US 5 (3.75 mm) needles.

Main hat
(*make 1*)
Using US 5 (3.75 mm) needles and A, cast on 16 sts.
Row 1: Inc1, k to last 2 sts, inc1, k1. (18 sts)
Row 2: Inc1 pwise, p to last 2 sts, inc1 pwise, p1. (20 sts)
Rep Rows 1-2 twice more. (24 sts)
Row 7: Cast on 30(33) sts, k to end. (54/57 sts)
Row 8: Cast on 30(33) sts, p to end. (84/90 sts)
Place a small safety pin marker at 26th(29th) st in from each edge.
Work 30(32) rows in st st beg with a k row.
Large size only:
Row 41: K4, [k2tog, k14] 5 times, k2tog, k4. (84 sts)
Row 42: P.
Both sizes:
Next row: K6, [k2tog, k12] 5 times, k2tog, k6. (78 sts)
Next and every WS row until stated otherwise: P.
Next RS row: K5, [sl1, k2tog, psso, k10] 5 times, sl1, k2tog, psso, k5. (66 sts)
Next RS row: K4, [sl1, k2tog, psso, k8] 5 times, sl1, k2tog, psso, k4. (54 sts)
Next RS row: K3, [sl1, k2tog, psso, k6] 5 times, sl1, k2tog, psso, k3. (42 sts)
Next RS row: K2, [sl1, k2tog, psso, k4] 5 times, sl1, k2tog, psso, k2. (30 sts)
Next RS row: K1, [sl1, k2tog, psso, k2] 5 times, sl1, k2tog, psso, k1. (18 sts)
Next row (WS): [P2tog] to end. (9 sts)
Break yarn leaving a long tail. Thread the tail through rem sts, pull up tightly and secure.

With RS facing and using A, pick up and k 26(29) sts across lower edge from RH edge towards first safety pin marker. Work 2 rows in st st beg with a p row.

Next row: P to last 2 sts, p2tog. (25/28 sts)
Next row: K2tog, k to end. (24/27 sts)
Next row: P to last 2 sts, p2tog. (23/26 sts)
Rep last 2 rows twice more. (19/22 sts)
Bind (cast) off.

With RS facing and using A, pick up and k 26(29) sts across lower edge from second safety pin marker to LH edge.
Work 2 rows in st st beg with a p row.
Next row: P2tog, p to end. (25/28 sts)
Next row: K to last 2 sts, ssk. (24/27 sts)
Next row: P2tog, p to end. (23/26 sts)
Rep last 2 rows twice more. (19/22 sts)
Bind (cast) off.

Eyes
(*make 2*)
Using US 3 (3.25 mm) needles and A, cast on 26 sts.
Row 1: K.
Row 2: [P2tog] to end. (13 sts)
Row 3: K.
Row 4: [P2tog] 3 times, k1, [p2tog] 3 times. (7 sts)

Break yarn, thread it through rem sts, pull up tightly and secure.

Making up and finishing
For general information on putting your hat together, see pages 104-107.

Join back seam of hat using flat-seam technique (see page 104).

Shape eye pieces into cup shapes with RS on inside and oversew seam. Turn pieces RS out. Stuff lightly and oversew eyes in place so seam runs down center of lowest part of eye. Using B, embroider a coil of chain stitch (see page 106) for center of each eye. Using C, embroider a circle of chain stitch round each eye center.

Using B, work nostrils and mouth in chain stitch.

Using the crochet hook and A, work a crochet edging (see page 107) around entire lower edge of hat, beginning and ending at back seam.

prickle the hedgehog

This spiny little mammal hat is made in a simple bobble stitch that's a breeze to knit once you're in the swing of it. Beady eyed with a cute round nose, this knitted version of the famous garden visitor is also guaranteed to be soft and cuddly—and 100% free of the pesky little fleas that love its real-life counterpart.

Main hat
(*make 1*)
Using US 9 (5.5 mm) needles and A, cast on 8 sts using yarn doubled.
Row 1: Inc1, k to last 2 sts, inc1, k1. (10 sts)
Row 2: P.
Rep Rows 1–2 once more. (12 sts)
Row 5: Cast on 6 sts in A, cast on 21(27) sts in Ball 1 of B, k21(27) sts in B, k18 sts in A. (39/45 sts)
Row 6: Cast on 6 sts in A; cast on 21(27) sts in Ball 1 of B, p21(27) sts in B, p18 sts in A, p21(27) sts in B. (66/78 sts)

Yarn
1 x ¾ oz (25 g) ball—approx 170 yds (155 m)—Sirdar Country Style DK in shade 409 Naturelle (A)
1(2) x 1¾ oz (50 g) ball(s)—each approx 170 yds (155 m) —Sirdar Country Style DK in shade 477 Mink (B)
Small amount of Sirdar Country Style DK in shade 417 Black (C)

You will also need
Sizes US 9 (5.5 mm) and US 3 (3.25 mm) knitting needles
Size US 7 (4.5 mm) crochet hook
Yarn sewing needle
Large-eyed embroidery needle

Sizes
3–10 years (11 years and over)

Actual measurements
Approx 16 in/41 cm (19½ in/49 cm) circumference

Gauge (tension)
16 sts and 21 rows to 4 in (10 cm) square over stockinette (stocking) stitch using yarn double on US 9 (5.5 mm) needles.

Special abbreviation
MB (make bobble)—k1, p1, k1 all into next st, turn work, p3. turn work again, slip 1, k2tog, psso (one bobble made)
decMB (decrease make bobble)—k2tog, [p1, k1] into same st, turn work, p3, turn work again, sl1, k2tog, psso.

Notes
Before you begin knitting, prepare two separate balls of B; Ball 1 consisting of 12 yds (11 m) of doubled yarn and Ball 2 consisting of 1 yd (0.9 m) of doubled yarn.

Work 2 rows in st st beg with a p row and cont A/B color patt as set.

Large size only:
Row 9: K4, [MB, k3] 5 times, MB, k2 in B; k24 in A; k2, [MB, k3] 5 times, MB, k4 in B.
Row 10: P27 in B, p24 in A, p27 in B.
Row 11: K2, [MB, k3] 5 times, MB, k4 in B; k24 in A; k4, [MB, k3] 5 times, MB, k2 in B.
Row 12: P27 in B, p24 in A, p27 in B.
Rep Rows 9-12 once more.
Row 17: K4, [MB, k3] 5 times, MB, k2 in B; k24 in A; k2, [MB, k3] 5 times, MB, k4 in B.
Row 18: P27 in B, p24 in A, p27 in B.
Row 19: K2, [MB, k3] 5 times, MB, k4 in B; k24 in A; k4, [MB, k3] 5 times, MB, k2 in B.
Row 20: P29 in B, p20 in A, p29 in B.
Row 21: K4, [MB, k3] 5 times, MB, k5 in B; k18 in A; k5, [MB, k3] 5 times, MB, k4 in B.
Row 22: P31 in B, p16 in A, p31 in B.
Row 23: K2, [MB, k3] 6 times, MB, k5 in B; k14 in A; k5, [MB, k3] 6 times, MB, k2 in B.
Row 24: P33 in B, p5 in A, join in Ball 2 of B, p2 in B; p5 in A, p33 in B.
Row 25: K4, [MB, k3] 6 times, MB, k5 in B; k3 in A; k4 in B; k3 in A; k5, [MB, k3] 6 times, MB, k4 in B.
Break off A and cont in B only.
Next and every WS row until stated otherwise: P.
Row 27 (RS): K2, [MB, k3] 9 times, k2tog, [k3, MB] 9 times, k2. (77 sts)

Small size only:
Row 9: K2, [MB, k3] 4 times, MB, k2 in B; k24 in A; k2, [MB, k3] 4 times, MB, k2 in B.
Row 10: P21 in B, p24 in A, p21 in B.
Row 11: K4, [MB, k3] 3 times, MB, k4 in B; k24 in A; k4, [MB, k3] 3 times, MB, k4 in B.
Row 12: P21 in B, p24 in A, p21 in B.
Row 13: K2, [MB, k3] 4 times, MB, k2 in B; k24 in A; k2, [MB, k3] 4 times, MB, k2 in B.

Row 14: P21 in B, p24 in A, p21 in B.
Row 15: K4, [MB, k3] 3 times, MB, k5 in B; k22 in A; k5, [MB, k3] 3 times, MB, k4 in B.
Row 16: P23 in B, p20 in A, p23 in B.
Row 17: K2, [MB, k3] 4 times, MB, k5 in B; k18 in A; k5, [MB, k3] 4 times, MB, k2 in B.
Row 18: P25 in B, p16 in A, p25 in B.
Row 19: K4, [MB, k3] 4 times, MB, k5 in B; k14 in A; k5, [MB, k3] 4 times, MB, k4 in B.
Row 20: P27 in B, p5 in A, join in Ball 2 of B, p2 in B, p5 in A, p27 in B.
Row 21: K2, [MB, k3] 5 times, MB, k5 in B; k3 in A; k4 in B; k3 in A; k5, [MB, k3] 5 times, MB, k2 in B.
Break off A and cont in B only.
Next and every WS row until stated otherwise: P.
Row 23 (RS): K4, [MB, k3] 6 times, k4, k2tog, k7, [MB, k3] 6 times, k1. (65 sts)

Both sizes:
Next RS row: K2(4), [MB, k3] to last 3(5) sts, MB, k2(4).
Next RS row: K4(2), [MB, k3] to last 5(3) sts, MB, k4(2).
Next RS row: K2(4), [MB, k3] to last 3(5) sts, MB, k2(4).

Large size only:
Row 35 (RS): K4, MB, [k2tog, k1, MB] 8 times, k3, [MB, k1, ssk] 8 times, MB, k4. (61 sts)
Row 37 (RS): K2, [decMB, k1] 9 times, k1, MB, k1, [k1, decMB] 9 times, k2. (43 sts)
Row 39 (RS): K4, [decMB, k2] 4 times, k3, [k2, decMB] 4 times, k4. (35 sts)

Small size only:
Row 31 (RS): K4, MB, [k2tog, k1, MB] 6 times, k3, MB, k3, [MB, k1, ssk] 6 times, MB, k4. (53 sts)
Row 33 (RS): K2, MB, k2, [decMB, k1] 6 times, k1, MB, k3, MB, k2, [decMB, k1] 6 times, k1, M1, k2. (41 sts)
Row 35 (RS): K4, MB, k1, [decMB, k1] 3 times, k1, MB, k3, MB, k3, MB, k2, [decMB, k1] 3 times, MB, k4. (35 sts)

Both sizes:
Next row (WS): [P2tog] 8 times, p3, [p2tog] 8 times. (19 sts)
Next row: K1, [k2tog] 4 times, k1, [ssk] 4 times, k1. (11 sts)
Next row: [P2tog] twice, p3, [p2tog] twice. (7 sts)
Break yarn leaving a long tail.
Thread the tail through rem sts, pull tightly and secure.

Ears
(*make 2*)
Using US 3 (3.25 mm) needles and A, cast on 10 sts.
Work 6 rows in st st beg with a k row.
Row 7: K1, k2tog, k to last 3 sts, ssk, k1. (8 sts)
Row 8: P.
Rep Rows 7-8 once more. (6 sts)
Row 11: K1, k2tog, ssk, k1. (4 sts)
Row 12: [P2tog] twice. (2 sts)
Row 13: [Inc1] twice. (4 sts)
Row 14: Inc1 pwise, p to last 2 sts, inc1 pwise, p1. (6 sts)
Row 15: K.
Rep Rows 14-15 twice more. (10 sts)
Work 4 rows in st st beg with a p row.
Bind (cast) off.

Making up and finishing

For general information on putting your hat together, see pages 104–107.

Join back seam of hat using the flat-seam technique (see page 104).

Fold ears in half widthwise RS together. Oversew round sides. Turn ears RS out and oversew lower edges. Stitch ears in place, forming a little pleat at front of ear as you sew.

Using C, embroider a small coil of chain stitch (see page 106) for each eye.

Using C, embroider a larger coil of chain stitch for nose.

Using the crochet hook and a single strand of A, work a crochet edging (see page 107) around entire lower edge of hat, beginning and ending at back seam.

savannah the zebra

With its striking monochrome stripes, the zebra is the design classic of the African plain. A little cuter than the real thing, this beast of a hat boasts some mighty cool stripes with a matching black and white mane. This hat is sure to drive any owner wild! See matching wrist warmers on page 37.

Yarn
1 x 1¾ oz (50g) ball–approx 109 yds (100 m)–Sirdar Country Style DK in shade 417 Black (A)
1 x 1¾ oz (50g) ball–approx 109 yds (100 m)–Sirdar Country Style DK in shade 412 White (B)
Small amount of Sirdar Country Style DK in shade 400 Silver gray (C)
Small amount of Katia Merino Blend DK in shade 25 Pale pink (D)

You will also need
Size US 9 (5.5 mm) knitting needles
Size US 7 (4.5 mm) crochet hook
Yarn sewing needle
Standard sewing needle
2 small safety pins

Sizes
3-10 years (11 years and over)

Actual measurements
Approx 15½ in/39 cm (18 in/46 cm) circumference

Gauge (tension)
17 sts and 21 rows to 4 in (10 cm) square over stockinette (stocking) stitch using yarn double on US 9 (5.5 mm) needles.

Notes
Before you begin knitting, prepare two separate balls of A; Ball 1 consisting of 1 yd (1 m) of doubled yarn and Ball 2 consisting of ½ yd (0.5 m) of doubled yarn. Prepare a separate ball of B yarn, Ball 3 consisting of 3 yds (3 m) of doubled yarn
Use doubled strands of yarn throughout.

Main hat
(*make 1*)
Using US 9 (5.5 mm) needles, cast on 66(78) sts in A from main ball, using yarn double.
Work 4 rows in st st beg with a k row. Break A.
Row 5: Join in Ball 3 of B, k28(34); join in Ball 1 of A, k10; join in main ball of B, k28(34).
Work 3 rows of st st beg with a p row and keeping to the B/A patt as set.
Leave B at side, rejoin main ball of A and work 4 rows in st st beg with a k row.
Row 13: K29(35) in B, join in Ball 2 of A, k8, k29(35) in B.
Row 14: P31(37) in B, p4 in A, p31(37) in B.
Break yarn from Ball 2 of A.
Work 2(4) rows in st st in B, beg with a k row.
Work 4 rows in st st in A, beg with a k row.
Work 4(6) rows in st st in B, beg with a k row.
Large size only:
Row 29: Cont in B, k5, [sl1, k2tog, psso, k10] 5 times, sl1, k2tog, psso, k5. (66 sts)
Row 30: P.
Both sizes:
Next row: Using A, k4, [k1, k2tog, pkso, k8] 5 times, k1, k2tog, pkso, k4. (54 sts)
Next and every WS row until stated otherwise: P, using same color yarn as previous RS row.
Next RS row: Cont in A, k3, [sl1, k2tog, psso, k6] 5 times, sl1, k2tog, psso, k3. (42 sts)
Next RS row: Using B, k2, [k1, k2tog, pkso, k4] 5 times, sl1, k2tog, psso, k2. (30 sts)

Before picking up stitches for the earflaps, fold the main hat piece together so the two short ends meet at the center. Place a small safety pin at each side of the hat at the cast-on edge to mark the center of each earflap. Pick up an equal number of stitches on either side of the marker for each earflap.

Tip

Next RS row: K1, [sl1, k2tog, psso, k2] 5 times, sl1, k2tog, psso, k11. (18 sts)
Next row (WS): [P2tog] to end. (9 sts)
Break yarn leaving a long tail.
Thread yarn tail through rem sts, pull tightly and secure.

Earflaps
(*make 2*)
With RS facing and using US 9 (5.5 mm) needles and a doubled strand of B, pick up and k 12(14) sts along cast-on edge for first earflap.
Work 3 rows in st st beg with a p row.
Leave B at side, join in two strands of A and work 4 rows of st st beg with a k row.

Leave A at side and work 2 rows of st st in B, beg with a k row.
Row 10: Using B, k1, k2tog, k to last 3 sts, ssk, k1. (10/12 sts)
Row 11: P (cont in color of previous row).
Rep last 4 rows once more in A, then once more in B. (6/8 sts)
Break B and cont in A only.
Work 2 rows in st st beg with a k row.
Large size only:
Row 22: K1, k2tog, k2, ssk, k1. (6 sts)
Row 23: P.
Both sizes:
Next row: K1, k2tog, ssk, K1. (4 sts)
Next row: [P2tog] twice. (2 sts)

Next row: K2tog. (1 st)
Break yarn and pull through rem st.
Work second earflap in the same way.

Ears
(*make 2*)
Using US 9 (5.5 mm) needles and B, cast on 16 sts using yarn double.
Work 2 rows in st st beg with a k row.
Row 3: K1, k2tog, k to last 3 sts, ssk, k1. (14 sts)
Row 4: P.
Rep Rows 3-4 four times more. (6 sts)
Row 13: K1, k2tog, ssk, k1. (4 sts)
Row 14: [P2tog] twice. (2 sts)
Row 15: K2tog. (1 st)
Break yarn and pull through rem st.

Making up and finishing
For general information on putting your hat together, see pages 104-107.

Join back seam of hat using flat-seam technique (see page 104).

Fold ear pieces in half lengthwise RS together. Oversew side seams. Turn ears RS out and oversew lower edge. Rep for second ear. Stitch ears in place with seams running down inside.

Using A, work a small coil of chain stitch (see page 106) for center of each eye. Using C, work a coil of chain stitch around each eye center.

Using D, embroider two small circles of chain stitch on nose area for nostrils.

For the mane, prepare three bunches of yarn, each consisting of 16 lengths of A, each length measuring 8 in (20 cm). Prepare another set using B. Join groups of yarn to top of hat, and down back, so A stripes have an A mane tuft and B stripes a B mane tuft. Begin at A stripe between ears. Use two bunches of B at top of hat where there is a double-width "stripe." Secure each group of yarn to hat by laying it flat and back stitching along center of yarn lengths, then straighten lengths and back stitch along lower edge, close to main hat.

Using the crochet hook and a doubled strand of A, work a crochet edging (see page 107) around entire lower edge of hat, including earflaps, beginning and ending at back seam.

savannah the zebra
wrist warmers

Wrist warmers are a simple and wonderful idea—and these zebra-striped ones will add a striking monochrome twist to any winter outfit. They're extra-super simple to knit and involve no shaping whatsoever. So if you're a budding knitter who is just getting going, this is the perfect first project.

Yarn
1 x 1¾ oz (50 g) ball—approx 109 yds (100 m)—Sirdar Country Style DK in shade 417 Black (A)
1 x 1¾ oz (50 g) ball—approx 109 yds (100 m)—Sirdar Country Style DK in shade 412 White (B)

You will also need
Size US 5 (3.75 mm) knitting needles
Yarn sewing needle

Sizes
7-10 years (11 years and over)

Actual measurements
Approx 3 in/8 cm (3½ in/9 cm) width laid flat

Gauge (tension)
23 sts and 30 rows to 4 in (10 cm) square over stockinette (stocking) stitch using US 5 (3.75 mm) needles.

Wrist warmer
(*make 2*)
Using US 5 (3.75 mm) needles and A, cast on 38(42) sts.
Row 1: [K2, p2] to last 2 sts, k2.
Row 2: [P2, k2] to last 2 sts, p2.
Rep first 2 rows 6 times more.
Leave A at side and join in B.
Work 4 rows in st st beg with a k row.
Leave B at side and pick up A.
Work 4 rows in st st beg with a k row.
Rep last 8 rows twice (3 times) more.
Leave A at side and pick up B.
Work 4 rows in st st beg with a k row.
Break B and cont in A only.
K 6 rows.
Bind (cast) off.

Making up and finishing
Sew seams using mattress stitch (see page 104).

boo the monster

You surely know a worthy recipient for this simple and speedy little monster hat. It's the perfect creation for using up that oddment of chunky yarn you've got hanging around—because this intrepid little fellow doesn't give a hoot about what color he's knitted in. Knit the basic hat and then unleash your creative side on his features to conjure up your own unique companion.

Yarn
1(2) x 1¾ oz (50 g) ball(s)—each approx 49 yds (45 m)—Sirdar Big Softie in shade 343 Bling blue (A)
Small amount of Sirdar Country Style DK in shade 417 Black (B)
Small pieces of lime green felt and gray marl felt
Lime green and black sewing threads
⅞ in (22 mm) pink button

You will also need
Size US 10.5 (6.5 mm) knitting needles
Yarn sewing needle
Large-eyed embroidery needle

Sizes
3-10 years (11 years and over)

Actual measurements
Approx 17¾ in/45 cm (20 in/50 cm) circumference

Gauge (tension)
12 sts and 17 rows to 4 in (10 cm) square over stockinette (stocking) stitch using US 10.5 (6.5 mm) needles.

Main hat
(*make 1*)
Using US 10.5 (6.5 mm) needles and A, cast on 54(60) sts.
K 4 rows.
Work 16(18) rows in st st beg with a K row.
Large size only:
Row 23: K4, [k2tog, k8] 3 times, [ssk, k8] twice, ssk, k4. (54 sts)
Row 24: P.
Both sizes:
Next row: K3, [sl1, k2tog, psso, k6] 5 times, sl1, k2tog, psso, k3. (42 sts)
Next and every WS row: P.
Next RS row: K2, [sl1, k2tog, psso, k4] 5 times, sl1, k2tog, psso, k2. (30 sts)
Next RS row: K1, [sl1, k2tog, psso, k2] 5 times, sl1, k2tog, psso, k1. (18 sts)
Next RS row: [sl1, k2tog, psso] 6 times. (6 sts)
Break yarn leaving a long tail.
Thread yarn tail through rem sts, pull up tightly and secure.

Horns
(*make 2*)
Using US 10.5 (6.5 mm) needles and A, cast on 4(6) sts.
Work 10 rows in st st beg with a k row.
Bind (cast) off.

Making up and finishing
For general information on putting your hat together, see pages 104-107.

Join back seam of hat using the flat-seam technique (see page 104).

Fold horn pieces in half lengthwise so RS on the outside. Oversew top and side seams. Stitch horns in place.

Using two strands of B, work a large cross stitch for one eye. Cut a circle of gray marl felt larger than the pink button for outer part of second eye and lay in place. Sew pink button through center of gray eye using black sewing thread, securing gray outer eye in place.

Cut a rectangle of lime green felt for nose. Using lime green sewing thread, oversew nose in place. Using B, work two straight stitches, one over the other, from bottom of nose to top of garter-stitch hat border.

squeak the mouse

Beady-eyed and ready for a quick nibble of cheese or chocolate, this sweet little mouse is the perfect head-topper for any girl who loves things a little pink and pretty. And as a bonus, the long earflaps will keep you extra warm— and it's great fun swinging those braids around too.

Yarn
2 x 1¾ oz (50 g) balls—each approx 79 yds (72 m)—
   Twilleys Freedom Purity Chunky in shade 781
   Clay (A)
Small amount of Katia Merino Blend DK in shade 25
   Pale Pink (B)
Small amount of Patons Diploma Gold DK in shade
   6183 Black (C)
Small amount of Patons Fairytale Dreamtime DK in
   shade 51 White (D)

You will also need
Size US 9 (5.5 mm) knitting needles
Size US D-3 (3.25 mm) crochet hook
Yarn sewing needle
Large-eyed embroidery needle
2 small safety pins

Sizes
3–10 years (11 years and over)

Actual measurements Approx 16 in/41 cm
(19½ in/49 cm) circumference

Gauge (tension)
16 sts and 22 rows to 4 in (10 cm) square over
   stockinette (stocking) stitch using US 9
   (5.5 mm) needles.

Hat
(*make 1*)
Using US 9 (5.5 mm) needles and A, cast on 8 sts.
Row 1: Inc1, k to last 2 sts, inc1, k1. (10 sts)
Row 2: P.
Rep Rows 1–2 once more. (12 sts)
Row 5: Cast on 27(33) sts, k to end. (39/45 sts)
Row 6: Cast on 27(33) sts, p to end. (66/78 sts)
Work 22(24) rows in st st beg with a k row.
Large size only:
Row 31: K5, [sl1, k2tog, psso, k10] 5 times, sl1, k2tog, psso,
k5. (66 sts)
Row 32: P.
Both sizes:
Next row: K4, [sl1, k2tog, psso, k8] 5 times, sl1, k2tog, psso,
k4. (54 sts)
Next and every WS row until stated otherwise: P.
Next RS row: K3, [sl1, k2tog, psso, k6] 5 times, sl1, k2tog,
psso, k3. (42 sts)
Next RS row: K2, [sl1, k2tog, psso, k4] 5 times, sl1, k2tog,
psso, k2. (30 sts)
Next RS row: K1, [sl1, k2tog, psso, k2] 5 times, sl1, k2tog,
psso, k1. (18 sts)
Next row (WS): [P2tog] to end. (9 sts)
Break yarn leaving a long tail.
Thread yarn tail through rem sts, pull up tightly
and secure.

Before picking up stitches for the earflaps, fold the main hat piece together so the two short ends meet at the center. Place a small safety pin at each side of the hat at the cast-on edge to mark the center of each earflap. Pick up an equal number of stitches on either side of the marker for each earflap.

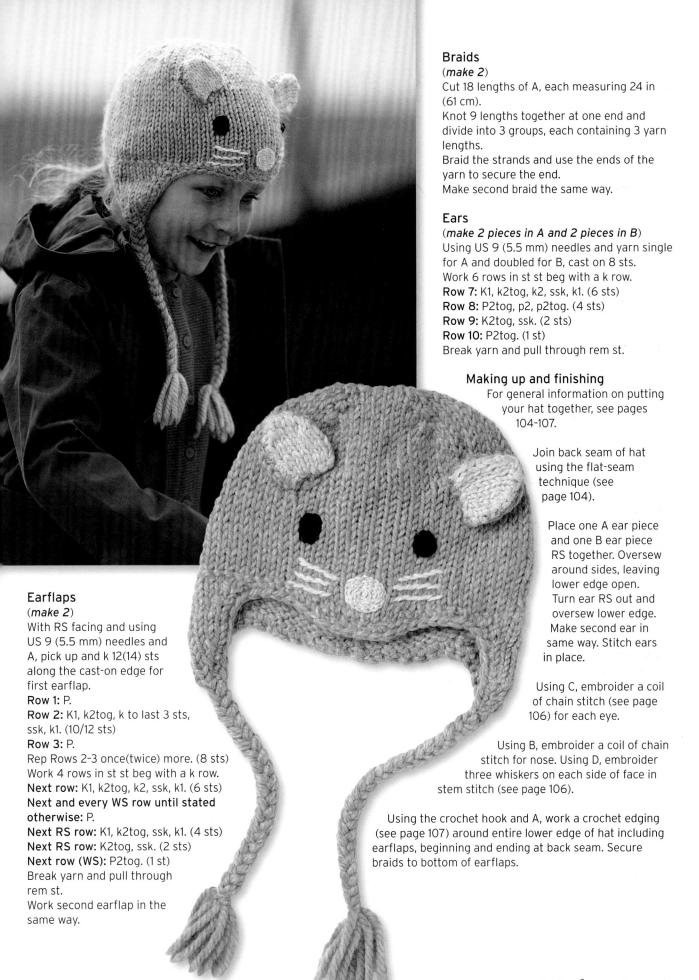

Braids
(*make 2*)
Cut 18 lengths of A, each measuring 24 in (61 cm).
Knot 9 lengths together at one end and divide into 3 groups, each containing 3 yarn lengths.
Braid the strands and use the ends of the yarn to secure the end.
Make second braid the same way.

Ears
(*make 2 pieces in A and 2 pieces in B*)
Using US 9 (5.5 mm) needles and yarn single for A and doubled for B, cast on 8 sts.
Work 6 rows in st st beg with a k row.
Row 7: K1, k2tog, k2, ssk, k1. (6 sts)
Row 8: P2tog, p2, p2tog. (4 sts)
Row 9: K2tog, ssk. (2 sts)
Row 10: P2tog. (1 st)
Break yarn and pull through rem st.

Making up and finishing
For general information on putting your hat together, see pages 104–107.

Join back seam of hat using the flat-seam technique (see page 104).

Place one A ear piece and one B ear piece RS together. Oversew around sides, leaving lower edge open. Turn ear RS out and oversew lower edge. Make second ear in same way. Stitch ears in place.

Using C, embroider a coil of chain stitch (see page 106) for each eye.

Using B, embroider a coil of chain stitch for nose. Using D, embroider three whiskers on each side of face in stem stitch (see page 106).

Using the crochet hook and A, work a crochet edging (see page 107) around entire lower edge of hat including earflaps, beginning and ending at back seam. Secure braids to bottom of earflaps.

Earflaps
(*make 2*)
With RS facing and using US 9 (5.5 mm) needles and A, pick up and k 12(14) sts along the cast-on edge for first earflap.
Row 1: P.
Row 2: K1, k2tog, k to last 3 sts, ssk, k1. (10/12 sts)
Row 3: P.
Rep Rows 2–3 once(twice) more. (8 sts)
Work 4 rows in st st beg with a k row.
Next row: K1, k2tog, k2, ssk, k1. (6 sts)
Next and every WS row until stated otherwise: P.
Next RS row: K1, k2tog, ssk, k1. (4 sts)
Next RS row: K2tog, ssk. (2 sts)
Next row (WS): P2tog. (1 st)
Break yarn and pull through rem st.
Work second earflap in the same way.

rumble bear

This traditional bear hat is knitted in an ultra-soft yarn on big needles, and the eyes and nose are made from felt, which means that as well as being one of the simplest patterns in the book, it is also probably the quickest to make. So now you have no excuses. Hit your local yarn store, grab yourself a couple of skeins... and click your needles into action.

Yarn
2 x 1¾ oz (50 g) balls—each approx 75 yds (80 m)— Wendy Norse Chunky in shade 2702 Eider (A)
Small amount of Sirdar Country Style DK in shade 417 Black (B)
Small amounts of black and cream felt
Cream and black sewing threads

You will also need
Sizes US 9 (5.5 mm) and US 10.5 (6.5 mm) knitting needles
Yarn sewing needle
Large-eyed embroidery needle
Standard sewing needle

Sizes
5-10 years (11 years and over)

Actual measurements
Approx 18½ in/47 cm (20 in/51 cm) circumference

Gauge (tension)
14 sts and 20 rows to 4 in (10 cm) square over stockinette (stocking) stitch using US 10.5 (6.5 mm) needles.

Main hat
(*make 1*)
Using US 9 (5.5 mm) needles and A, cast on 66(72) sts.
K 4 rows.
Change to US 10.5 (6.5 mm) needles.
Work 22(28) rows in st st beg with a k row.
Large size only:
Row 33: K5, [k2tog, k10] 3 times, [ssk, k10] twice, ssk, k5. (66 sts)
Row 34: P.
Both sizes:
Next row: [sl1, k2tog, psso, k8] 5 times, sl1, k2tog, psso, k4. (54 sts)
Next and every WS row: P.
Next RS row: K3, [sl1, k2tog, psso, k6] 5 times, sl1, k2tog, psso, k3. (42 sts)
Next RS row: K2, [sl1, k2tog, psso, k4] 5 times, sl1, k2tog, psso, k2. (30 sts)
Next RS row: K1, [sl1, k2tog, psso, k2] 5 times, sl1, k2tog, psso, k1. (18 sts)

Next RS row: [sl1, k2tog, psso] 6 times. (6 sts)
Break yarn leaving a long tail.
Thread the tail through rem sts, pull up tightly and secure.

Ears
(*make 2*)
Using US 10.5 (6.5 mm) needles and A, cast on 8 sts.
Work 5 rows in st st beg with a k row.
Row 6: P2tog, p4, p2tog. (6 sts)
Row 7: K2tog, k2, ssk. (4 sts)
Row 8: [P2tog] twice. (2 sts)
Row 9: [Inc1] twice. (4 sts)
Row 10: [Inc1 pwise, p1] twice. (6 sts)
Row 11: Inc1, k3, inc1, k1. (8 sts)
Work 4 rows in st st beg with a p row.
Bind (cast) off kwise on WS of work.

Making up and finishing
For general information on putting your hat together, see pages 104–107.

Join back seam of hat using the flat-seam technique (see page 104).

Fold ear pieces in half widthwise RS together so cast-on and bound- (cast-) off edges meet. Oversew around curved edges then turn ears RS out. Oversew lower edges. Stitch ears in place.

Cut two circles measuring ³/₄ in (1.9 cm) in diameter in black felt for the eyes. Cut an oval shape measuring 2³/₄ in (7 cm) lengthwise in cream felt for the muzzle. Cut a rounded triangle measuring 1 in (2.5 cm) along its straight edge in black felt for the nose.

Using B, secure eyes in place with a French knot (see page 106). Using cream thread, work a row of small running stitches round muzzle, close to edge, to secure in place. Oversew nose on muzzle using black thread.

Using B, work a row of chain stitch (see page 106) from nose to bottom of muzzle.

rumble bear mittens

These chunky fingerless mittens will keep small hands warm and cozy, while allowing little fingers to wriggle free. They are also one of the quickest items to knit and finish in the whole book. We've knitted them in a soft brown to tone with the bear hat on page 43, but you could knit them in any shade that takes your fancy.

Yarn
1 x 1¾ oz (50 g) ball–approx 49 yds (45 m)–of
   Sirdar Big Softie in shade 326 Moose (A)
Small amount of Sirdar Country Style DK in shade
   530 Chocolate (B)

You will also need
Size US 10.5 (6.5 mm) knitting needles
Yarn sewing needle
Large-eyed embroidery needle

Sizes
7-10 years (11 years and over)

Actual measurements
Approx 3¼ in/8 cm (4 in/10 cm) width laid flat

Gauge (tension)
12 sts and 17 rows to
   4 in (10 cm) square
   over stockinette
   (stocking) stitch
   using US 10.5
   (6.5 mm) needles.

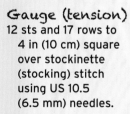

Mittens
(*make 2*)
Using US 10.5 (6.5 mm) needles and A, cast on 20(24) sts.
Row 1: [K2, p2] to end.
Rep first row 9 times more.
Work 12(14) rows in st st beg with a k row.
Next row: [K2, p2] to end.
Rep last row 3 times more.
Bind (cast) off keeping to the k2, p2 pattern.

Making up and finishing
Sew seams of mittens using the flat-seam technique (see page 104), leaving a 1½ in/4 cm (2 in/5 cm) gap just above the ribbing at each wrist for the thumb to go through.

Using a doubled strand of B, work an oval of chain stitch (see page 106) on the palm of each mitten for the paw pad–remembering that the thumb hole for one mitten should be on the right and the thumb hole for the second mitten should be on the left.

Using B, work four French knots (see page 106) just above top edge of oval, winding yarn round the needle 3 times instead of the normal twice for each knot.

otto the octopus

Eight arms are better than two—at least if you are an octopus and need to twirl your arms around your prey to procure a decent meal. Knitted here in bright pink yarn—hardly the ideal camouflage—this octo-hat will not make you move by jet propulsion like a real-life octopus or, for that matter, help you to squeeze into a tight corner. But, in any case, in this headgear you'll want to hang around and get noticed.

Yarn
2 x 1¾ oz (50 g) balls—each approx 109 yds (100 m)—Sirdar Country Style DK in shade 527 Rosehip (A)
Small amount of Patons Diploma Gold DK in shade 6183 Black (B)
Small amount of Patons Fairytale Dreamtime DK in shade 51 White (C)

You will also need
Size US 9 (5.5 mm) knitting needles
Size US J-10 (6 mm) crochet hook
Yarn sewing needle
Large-eyed embroidery needle

Sizes
3-10 years (11+ years)

Actual measurements
Approx 17 in/43 cm (20 in/51 cm) circumference

Gauge (tension)
16 sts and 22 rows to 4 in (10 cm) square over stockinette (stocking) stitch using yarn double on US 9 (5.5 mm) needles.

Main hat
(*make 1*)
Using US 9 (5.5 mm) needles and A double, cast on 66(78) sts.
Place a small safety pin marker on 23rd(26th) st in from each edge.
K 4 rows.
Work 22(26) rows in st st beg with a k row.
Large size only:
Row 31: K5, [sl1, k2tog, psso, k10] 5 times, sl1, k2tog, psso, k5. (66 sts)
Row 32: P.
Both sizes:
Next row: K4, [sl1, k2tog, psso, k8] 5 times, sl1, k2tog, psso, k4. (54 sts)
Next and every WS row until stated otherwise: P.
Next RS row: K3, [sl1, k2tog, psso, k6] 5 times, sl1, k2tog, psso, k3. (42 sts)
Next RS row: K2, [sl1, k2tog, psso, k4] 5 times, sl1, k2tog, psso, k2. (30 sts)
Next RS row: K1, [sl1, k2tog, psso, k2] 5 times, sl1, k2tog, psso, k1. (18 sts)
Next row (WS): [P2tog] to end. (9 sts)
Break yarn leaving a long tail. Thread yarn tail through rem sts, pull up tightly and secure.

With RS of work facing and using A double, pick up and k 23(26) sts across lower edge from RH edge toward first safety pin marker.
Next row: K.
Next row: K to last 2 sts, k2tog. (22/25 sts)
Rep last 2 rows twice (3 times) more. (20/22 sts)
Bind (cast) off.

With RS of work facing and using a doubled strand of A, pick up and k 23(26) sts across lower edge from second safety pin marker to LH edge.

Next row: K.
Next row: Ssk, k to end. (22/25 sts)
Rep last 2 rows 2(3) times more. (20/22 sts)
Bind (cast) off.

Tentacles

Measure 8 lengths of A, each measuring 8½ yds (7.5 m). Fold each length in half, then in half again twice more; each length will now consist of eight strands of yarn. Using the crochet hook, work eight 6¼ in (16 cm) crochet chains. Trim ends of yarn to 1 in (2.5 cm).

Making up and finishing

For general information on putting your hat together, see pages 104–107.

Join back seam of hat using the flat-seam technique (see page 104).

Using a doubled strand of B, work two French knots (see page 106) for eyes. Using C, embroider three circles of chain stitch (see page 106) around each French knot.

Using B, work a 2½ in (6 cm) row of chain stitch for mouth.

Sew one tentacle at each side of lower edge of hat. Space other tentacles evenly between them, securing with eight strands of yarn.

waddle the penguin

skill level

If you fancy a bit of tobogganing on the snow, nothing could be more perfect than this penguin hat. The soft, super chunky yarn will make sure you keep warm—and you'll also look right at home messing around on the slopes. If you fancy a snack of raw fish, feel free. But if a bowl of soup or a mug of hot chocolate is more your sort of thing, then that's OK, too.

Yarn
1(2) x 1¾ oz (50 g) ball(s)—each approx 49 yds (45 m)—Sirdar Big Softie in shade 338 Kitten (A)
1 x 1¾ oz (50 g) ball—approx 49 yds (45 m)—Sirdar Big Softie in each of shade 330 Meringue (B) and shade 320 Tangerine (C)
Small amounts of Sirdar Country Style DK in shade 417 Black (D) and shade 400 Silver Gray (E)

You will also need
Size US 10.5 (6.5 mm) knitting needles
Yarn sewing needle
Large-eyed embroidery needle
2 small safety pins

Sizes
3-10 years (11 years and over)

Actual measurements
Approx 17¾ in/45 cm (20 in/50 cm) circumference

Gauge (tension)
12 sts and 17 rows to 4 in (10 cm) square over stockinette (stocking) stitch using US 10.5 (6.5 mm) needles.

Notes
Before you begin knitting, prepare two separate balls of A; Ball 1 consisting of 13 yds (12 m) of yarn and Ball 2 consisting of 1 yd (1 m) of yarn.

Main hat
(*make 1*)
Using US 10.5 (6.5 mm) needles, cast on 19(22) sts in Ball 1 of A, 16 sts in B, and 19(22) sts in main ball of A. (54/60 sts)
Row 1: [K1, p1] to end, keeping to A/B patt as set.
Row 2: [P1, k1] to end, keeping to A/B patt as set.
Keeping to A/B patt as set, work 7 rows in st st beg with a k row.
Row 10: P20(23) in A, p14 in B, p20(23) in A.
Row 11: K21(24) in A, k5 in B, join in Ball 2 of A, k2 in A, k5 in B, k21(24) in A.
Row 12: P22(25) in A, p3 in B, p4 in A, p3 in B, p22(25) in A.
Cont in A only, break all yarns no longer in use.
Work 8(10) rows in st st beg with a k row.
Large size only:
Row 23: K4, [k2tog, k8] 3 times, [ssk, k8] twice, ssk, k4. (54 sts)

Before picking up stitches for the earflaps, fold the main hat piece together, so the two short ends meet at the center. Place a small safety pin at each side of the hat at the cast-on edge to mark the center of each earflap. Pick up an equal number of stitches on either side of the marker for each earflap.

Tip

Row 24: P.
Both sizes:
Next row: K3, [sl1, k2tog, psso, k6] 5 times, sl1, k2tog, psso, k3. (42 sts)
Next and every WS row: P.
Next RS row: K2, [sl1, k2tog, psso, k4] 5 times, sl1, k2tog, psso, k2. (30 sts)
Next RS row: K1, [sl1, k2tog, psso, k2] 5 times, sl1, k2tog, psso, k1. (18 sts)
Next row: P.
Next row: [sl1, k2tog, psso] 6 times. (6 sts)
Break yarn leaving a long tail.
Thread yarn tail through rem sts, pull up tightly and secure.

Earflaps
(*make 2*)
With RS facing and using US 10 (6.5 mm) needles and A, pick up and k 9(11) sts along cast-on edge for first earflap.
Row 1: [K1, p1] to last st, k1.
Rep first row once(3 times) more.
Next row: P2tog, [k1, p1] twice(3 times), k1, p2tog. (7/9 sts)
Next row: [P1, k1] 3(4) times, p1.
Rep last row twice more.
Large size only:
Next row: K2tog, [p1, k1] twice, p1, k2tog. (7 sts)
Both sizes:
Next row: P2tog, k1, p1, k1, p2tog. (5 sts)
Next row: K2tog, p1, k2tog. (3 sts)
Next row: P2tog, k1, p2tog. (1 st)
Break yarn and pull through rem st.
Work second earflap in the same way.

Beak peak
Using C, pick up and k 14 sts across lower edge of white part of face (there are 16 sts, so skip 2nd and 15th sts). (14 sts)
Row 1: P2tog, p to last 2 sts, p2tog. (12 sts)
Row 2: K1, ssk, k to last 3 sts, k2tog, k1. (10 sts)
Row 3: P2tog, p to last 2 sts, p2tog. (8 sts)
Row 4: K1, ssk, k2, k2tog, k1. (6 sts)
Row 5: Inc1 pwise, p to last 2 sts, inc1 pwise, p1. (8 sts)

Row 6: Inc1, k to last 2 sts, inc1, k1. (10 sts)
Rep Rows 5-6 once more. (14 sts)
Bind (cast) off kwise on WS of work.

Making up and finishing
For general information on putting your hat together, see pages 104–107.

Join back seam of hat using the flat-seam technique (see page 104).

Fold lower edge of beak upward so upper and lower parts are RS together. Oversew sides of beak. Turn beak RS out and oversew bound- (cast-) off edge (now on underside of beak) to cast-on edge on inside of face.

Using D, embroider a coil of chain stitch (see page 106) for each eye center. Using E, embroider a circle of chain stitch round each eye center.

nana the monkey

This is the ideal hat to knit for the pesky little monkey—or little monkeys—in your life. It's knitted here in a monkey-ish shade of brown but it would work really well in a soft gray, too. And if you want a sock-monkey look, try knitting it in a tweedy gray and give her (or him) a red mouth. Please don't be put off by the cream face—it is much easier to knit than it looks.

Yarn
1(2) x 1¾ oz (50 g) ball(s)—each approx 127 yds
  (116 m)—Wendy Merino DK in shade 2381 Otter (A)
1 x 1¾ oz (50 g) ball—approx 109 yds (100 m)—Sirdar
  Country Style DK in shade 411 Cream (B)
Small amount of Sirdar Country Style DK in shade
  417 Black (C)
Small amount of Patons Diploma Gold DK in shade
  6184 Steel (D)
Small amount of Katia Merino Blend DK in shade 25
  Pale Pink (E)
Small amount of Wendy Merino DK in shade 2370
  Fuchsia (F)

You will also need
Size US 9 (5.5 mm) knitting needles
Yarn sewing needle
Large-eyed embroidery needle

Size
3-10 years (11+ years)

Actual measurements
Approx 16 in/41 cm (19½ in/49 cm) circumference

Gauge (tension)
16 sts and 22 rows to 4 in (10 cm) square over
  stockinette (stocking) stitch using yarn double
  on US 9 (5.5 mm) needles.

Notes
Before you begin knitting, prepare a small ball of
A consisting of 17 yds (16 m) of doubled yarn.

Main hat
(*make 1*)
Using US 9 (5.5 mm) needles, cast on 22(28) sts from small ball of A using yarn double, 22 sts in B using yarn double, and 22(28) sts in A from main ball using yarn double.
Row 1: [K2, p2] to last 2 sts, keeping to A/B patt as set, k2.
Row 2: [P2, k2] to last 2 sts, keeping to A/B patt as set, p2.
Rep Rows 1-2 once more.
Work 10(12) rows in st st beg with a k row, keeping to A/B patt as set.
Next row: K23(29) in A, k9 in B, k2 in A, k9 in B, k23(29) in A.
Next row: P24(30) in A, p7 in B, p4 in A, p7 in B, p24(30) in A.
Next row: K25(31) in A, k5 in B, k6 in A, k5 in B, k25(31) in A.
Cont in A, breaking yarns no longer in use.
Work 11(13) rows in st st beg with a p row.
Large size only:
Row 33: K5, [sl1, k2tog, psso, k10] 5 times, sl1, k2tog, psso, k5. (66 sts)
Row 34: P.
Both sizes:
Next row: K4, [sl1, k2tog, psso, k8] 5 times, sl1, k2tog, psso, k4. (54 sts)
Next and every WS row until stated otherwise: P.
Next RS row: K3, [sl1, k2tog, psso, k6] 5 times, sl1, k2tog, psso, k3. (42 sts)
Next RS row: K2, [sl1, k2tog, psso, k4] 5 times, sl1, k2tog, psso, k2. (30 sts)
Next RS row: K1, [sl1, k2tog, psso, k2] 5 times, sl1, k2tog, psso, k1. (18 sts)
Next row (WS): [P2tog] to end. (9 sts)
Break yarn, thread through rem sts and secure.

Ears
(*make 2*)
Using size US 9 (5.5 mm) needles and a double strand of A, cast on 5 sts.
Row 1: Inc1, k2, inc1, k1. (7 sts)
Row 2: P.
Row 3: Inc1, k to last 2 sts, inc1, k1. (9 sts)

Row 4: P.
Rep Rows 3-4 once more. (11 sts)
Work 4 rows in st st beg with a k row.
Row 11: K1, k2tog, k to last 3 sts, ssk, k1. (9 sts)
Row 12: P.
Rep Rows 11-12 once more. (7 sts)
Bind (cast) off.

Making up and finishing

For general information on putting your hat together, see pages 104-107.

Join back seam of hat using the flat-seam technique (see page 104).

Fold ear pieces in half RS together so cast-on and bound-(cast-) off edges meet. Oversew around curved sides, leaving flat part open for turning. Turn ears RS out and close gap using mattress stitch (see page 104). Stitch ears in place on side of hat.

Using doubled strand of C, work two French knots (see page 106) for eyes. Using D, embroider a few circles of chain stitch (see page 106) around each French knot.

Using E, embroider two small circles of chain stitch for nostrils.

Using F, work a line of chain stitch for mouth.

gurgle the fish

With its swishing tail and jaunty fins—and a mouth big enough to trap a human head—this is one seriously eye-catching hat. It's knitted here in bright turquoise throughout, but you could knit it in any color that takes your fancy; knit the fish in bright orange for a goldfish fancier, or in stripes for a Mexican festival feel. Just knit him!

Yarn
2 x 1¾ oz (50 g) balls—approx 49 yds (45 m)—Sirdar Big Softie in shade 348 Rich Turquoise (A)
Small amount of Sirdar Country Style DK in shade 527 Rosehip (B), shade 417 Black (C), and shade 412 White (D)

You will also need
Size US 10.5 (6.5 mm) knitting needles
Yarn sewing needle
Large-eyed embroidery needle
2 small safety pins

Sizes
3-10 years (11 years and over)

Actual measurements
Approx 17¾ in/45 cm (20 in/50 cm) circumference

Gauge (tension)
12 sts and 17 rows to 4 in (10 cm) square over stockinette (stocking) stitch using US 10.5 (6.5 mm) needles.

Main hat
(*make 1*)
Using US 10.5 (6.5 mm) needles and A, cast on 54(60) sts. Place small safety pin marker at 24th st in from each edge. Work 18(20) rows in st st beg with a K row.
Large size only:
Row 21: K4, [k2tog, k8] 3 times, [ssk, k8] twice, ssk, k4. (54 sts)
Row 22: P.
Both sizes:
Next row: K3, [sl1, k2tog, psso, k6] 5 times, sl1, k2tog, psso, k3. (42 sts)
Next row: P.
Next row: K2, [sl1, k2tog, psso, k4] 5 times, sl1, k2tog, psso, k2. (30 sts)
Next row: P.
Next row: K2, [k2tog, k3] twice, k2tog, k2, [ssk, k3] twice, ssk, k2. (24 sts)
Work 5 rows in st st beg with a p row.
Next row: K1, [k2tog, k2] 3 times, [ssk, k2] twice, ssk, k1. (18 sts)
Work 5 rows in st st beg with a p row.
Next row: K1, [k2tog, k1] twice, k2tog, [ssk, k1] 3 times. (12 sts)
Work 7 rows in st st beg with a p row.
Next row: K3, M1, k6, M1, k3. (14 sts)
Next and every WS row: P.
Next RS row: K3, M1, k1, M1, k8, M1, k1, M1, k3. (18 sts)
Next RS row: K4, M1, k1, M1, k8, M1, k1, M1, k4. (22 sts)
Next RS row: K5, M1, k1, M1, k10, M1, k1, M1, k5. (26 sts)
Next row: P.
Bind (cast) off.

With RS of work facing and using A, pick up and k 24 sts across lower edge from RH edge to first safety pin marker.
Next row: P2tog, p to end. (23 sts)
Next row: K to last 2 sts, ssk. (22 sts)
Rep last 2 rows once more. (20 sts)
Next row: P2tog, p to end. (19 sts)
Bind (cast) off.

With RS of work facing and using A, pick up and k 24 sts across lower edge from second safety pin marker to LH edge.
Next row: P to last 2 sts, p2tog. (23 sts)

Next row: K2tog, k to end. (22 sts)
Rep last 2 rows once more. (20 sts)
Next row: P to last 2 sts, p2tog. (19 sts)
Bind (cast) off.

Fins
(*make 2*)
Using US 10.5 (6.5 mm) needles and
A, cast on 8 sts.
Row 1: Inc1, k to last 2 sts, inc1, k1.
(10 sts)
Row 2: K1, p to last st, k1.
Rep Rows 1–2 once more. (12 sts)
Row 5: K.
Row 6: K1, p to last st, k1.
Rep Rows 5–6 once more.
K 2 rows.
Bind (cast) off.

Making up and finishing
For general information on
putting your hat together, see
pages 104–107.

Join back seam of hat using
the flat-seam technique (see
page 104). With hat inside out,
oversew across bottom of tail.
Turn hat RS out.

With RS of hat facing and using three strands of B, pick up
and k 19(25) sts along lower front edge of hat, from one
edge of lower part of hat, up side, across cast-on edge, and
down other side.
Next row: P.
Bind (cast) off.

Oversew fins in place across base of each fin, on front of
hat as shown.

Using C, embroider a coil of chain stitch (see page 106) for
each eye center. Using D, work three circles of chain stitch
round each eye center.

leandro the lion

Powerful and loud—though admittedly rather lazy—lions are magnificent creatures. Knitted in soft golden yarn with a rust crochet-chain mane, this fabulous feline is the perfect hat to knit for your own little king of the jungle. Get your needles clicking and stand back to watch him roar.

Yarn
2 x 1¾ oz (50 g) balls—each approx 109 yds (100 m) —Sirdar Country Style DK in shade 399 Gold (A)
1 x 3½ oz (100 g) ball—approx 218 yds (200 m)— Rowan Creative Focus Worsted in shade 02190 Copper (B)
Small amounts of Sirdar Country Style DK in shade 417 Black (C) and shade 412 White (D)
½ in (13 mm) snap fastener
¾ in (15 mm) yellow/brown button
Sewing thread to match the gold yarn

You will also need
Sizes US 9 (5.5 mm) and US 3 (3.25 mm) knitting needles
Size US 7 (4.5 mm) crochet hook
Yarn sewing needle
Large-eyed embroidery needle
Standard sewing needle
2 small safety pins

Size
3-10 years

Actual measurements
Approx 16 in/41 cm circumference

Gauge (tension)
16 sts and 22 rows to 4 in (10 cm) square over stockinette (stocking) stitch using yarn double on US 9 (5.5 mm) needles.

Main hat
(*make 1*)
Using US 9 (5.5 mm) needles and A, cast on 66 sts using yarn double.
Place a small safety pin marker at 26th st in on each edge.
Row 1: [K1, p1] to end.
Row 2: [P1, k1] to end.
Work 18 rows in st st beg with a k row.
Row 21: K4, [sl1, k2tog, psso, k8] 5 times, sl1, k2tog, psso, k4. (54 sts)
Row 22 every WS row until stated: P.
Row 23 (RS): K3, [sl1, k2tog, psso, k6] 5 times, sl1, k2tog, psso, k3. (42 sts)
Row 25 (RS): K2, [sl1, k2tog, psso, k4] 5 times, sl1, k2tog, psso, k2. (30 sts)
Row 27 (RS): K1, [sl1, k2tog, psso, k2] 5 times, sl1, k2tog, psso, k1. (18 sts)
Row 28 (WS): [P2tog] to end. (9 sts)
Break yarn leaving a long tail.
Thread the tail through rem sts, pull up tightly and secure.

With RS of work facing and using A, pick up and k 26 sts across lower edge from RH edge toward first safety pin marker.
Next row: K2tog, [p1, k1] to end. (25 sts)
Next row: [K1, p1] to last 3 sts, k1, p2tog. (24 sts)
Rep last 2 rows once more. (22 sts)
Next row: K2tog, [p1, k1] to end. (21 sts)
Next row: Bind (cast) off 8 sts, [p1, k1] to end. (13 sts)
Next row: [K1, p1] to last 3 sts, k1, p2tog. (12 sts)
Next row: [P1, k1] to end.
Next row: [K1, p1] to end.
*****Next row:** K2tog, [p1, k1] to last 2 sts, p2tog. (10 sts)
Next row: [P1, k1] to end.
Next row: P2tog, [k1, p1] to last 2 sts, k2tog. (8 sts)
Next row: [K1, p1] to end.
Next row: K2tog, [p1, k1] twice, p2tog. (6 sts)
Next row: [P1, k1] to end.
Next row: P2tog, k1, p1, k2tog. (4 sts)
Next row: [K1, p1] twice.
Next row: [P1, k1] twice.
Rep last 2 rows 10 times more.
Bind (cast) off kwise**, leaving a long tail.

With the crochet hook, use yarn tail to make a short chain to form button loop.

With RS of work facing and using A, pick up and k 26 sts across lower edge from second safety pin marker to LH edge.

Next row: [K1, p1] to last 2 sts, ssk. (25 sts)
Next row: P2tog, k1, [p1, k1] to end. (24 sts)
Next row: [K1, p1] to last 2 sts, ssk. (23 sts)
Next row: P2tog, k1, [p1, k1] to end. (22 sts)
Next row: [K1, p1] to last 2 sts, ssk. (21 sts)
Next row: [K1, p1] 6 times, k1, bind (cast) off rem sts. (13 sts)
Break yarn and rejoin it to rem sts on WS of work.
Next row: [K1, p1] to last 3 sts, k1, p2tog. (12 sts)
Next row: [P1, k1] to end.
Next row: [K1, p1] to end.
Cont as for other side from * to **.

Ears
(*make 2*)
Using US 9 (5.5 mm) needles and A, cast on 10 sts using yarn double.
Work 6 rows in st st beg with a k row.
Row 7: K2tog, k6, ssk. (8 sts)

Row 8: P2tog, p4, p2tog. (6 sts)
Row 9: K2tog, k2, ssk. (4 sts)
Row 10: [P2tog] twice. (2 sts)
Row 11: [Inc1] twice. (4 sts)
Row 12: [Inc1 pwise, p1] twice. (6 sts)
Row 13: Inc1, k3, inc1, k1. (8 sts)
Row 14: Inc1 pwise, p5, inc1 pwise, p1.
(10 sts)
Work 5 rows in st st beg with a k row.
Bind (cast) off kwise.

Nose
(*make 1*)
Using US 3 (3.25 mm) needles and C, cast
on 12 sts.
Work 2 rows in st st beg with a k row.
Row 3: K2tog, k8, ssk. (10 sts)
Row 4: P2tog, p6, p2tog. (8 sts)
Row 5: K2tog, k4, ssk. (6 sts)
Row 6: P2tog, p2, p2tog. (4 sts)
Row 7: K2tog, ssk. (2 sts)
Row 8: P2tog.
Break yarn and pull through rem st.

Mane
Using the crochet hook, work a 3 yd
(2.5 m) chain in B. Leave last st on hook
until ready to sew mane onto hat.

Making up and finishing
For general information on putting your
hat together, see pages 104-107.

Join back of hat using the flat-seam
technique (see page 104).

Join loose end of crochet chain for button
loop to RH corner of hat strap.

Fold ears in half widthwise RS together.
Oversew sides. Turn ear RS out and
oversew lower edges. Stitch ears in place.

Oversew nose in place. Using C, work a
short row of chain stitch (see page 106)
from nose down to top of seed (moss)
stitch border.

Using C, embroider a small coil of chain
stitch for each eye center. Using D,
embroider two circles of chain stitch round
eye centers.

Using B, back stitch mane in place around sides and top
of hat; it should run just behind ears and loops of mane
should be about 1¼ in (3 cm) long. If necessary, undo
a little chain or work a little more so mane fits round
hat exactly.

Place strap end with loop over other strap end to overlap
by 2¾ in (7 cm). Sew button in place. Sew lower part of
snap fastener to upper side of lower strap and top part
of snap fastener to corresponding position on underside
of top strap.

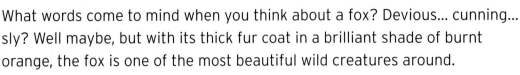

rusty the fox

What words come to mind when you think about a fox? Devious... cunning... sly? Well maybe, but with its thick fur coat in a brilliant shade of burnt orange, the fox is one of the most beautiful wild creatures around. Straightforward to knit and with long earflaps to keep the wind out, this foxy hat is a wardrobe essential for the fall. Just keep it away from the cute chick hat on page 10.

Yarn
1 x 1¾ oz (50 g) ball—approx 191 yds (175 m)—Rowan Felted Tweed DK in shade 154 Ginger (A)
1 x 1¾ oz (50 g) ball—approx 98 yds (90 m)—Patons Fairytale Dreamtime DK in shade 51 White (B)
Small amount of Sirdar Country Style DK in shade 417 Black (C)

You will also need
Sizes US 9 (5.5 mm) and US 3 (3.25 mm) knitting needles
Yarn sewing needle
Large-eyed embroidery needle
2 small safety pins

Sizes
3–10 years (11 years and over)

Actual measurements
Approx 15¼ in/39 cm (18 in/46 cm) circumference

Gauge (tension)
17 sts and 24 rows to 4 in (10 cm) square over stockinette (stocking) stitch using yarn double on US 9 (5.5 mm) needles.

Notes
Before you begin knitting, prepare two separate balls of A; Ball 1 consisting of 16½ yds (15 m) of doubled yarn and Ball 2 consisting of 2½ yds (2 m) of doubled yarn.
  For the hat and ears, use doubled strands of yarn throughout.

Main hat
(*make 1*)
Using US 9 (5.5 mm) needles, cast on 20(26) sts in Ball 1 of A, 26 sts in double strand of B, and 20(26) sts from main ball of A, using yarn double. (66/78 sts)
K 4 rows keeping to A/B patt as set.
Work 6(8) rows in st st beg with a k row.
Next row: K20(26) in A, k12 in B, join in Ball 2 of A, k2 in A, k12 in B, k20(26) in A.
Next row: P20(26) in A, p11 in B, p4 in A, p11 in B, p20(26) in A.
Next row: K20(26) in A, k10 in B, k6 in A, k10 in B, k20(26) in A.
Next row: P20(26) in A, p9 in B, p8 in A, p9 in B, p20(26) in A.
Break off B, cont in A only.
Work 10(12) rows in st st beg with a k row.
Large size only:
Next row: K5, [sl1, k2tog, psso, k10] 5 times, sl1, k2tog, psso, k5. (66 sts)
Next row: P
Both sizes:
Next row: K4, [sl1, k2tog, psso, k8] 5 times, sl1, k2tog, psso, k4. (54 sts)
Next and every WS row until stated otherwise: P.
Next RS row: K3, [sl1, k2tog, psso, k6] 5 times, sl1, k2tog, psso, k3. (42 sts)
Next RS row: K2, [sl1, k2tog, psso, k4] 5 times, sl1, k2tog, psso, k2. (30 sts)
Next RS row: K1, [sl1, k2tog, psso, k2] 5 times, sl1, k2tog, psso, k1. (18 sts)
Next row (WS): [P2tog] to end. (9 sts)
Break yarn leaving a long tail.
Thread the tail through rem sts, pull up tightly and secure.

Ears

(*make 2 pieces in A and 2 pieces in B*)

With US 9 (5.5 mm) needles and yarn doubled, cast on 12 sts.

Work 4 rows in st st beg with a k row.

Row 5: K1, k2tog, k to last 3 sts, ssk, k1. (10 sts)

Row 6: P.

Rep last 2 rows twice more. (6 sts)

Row 11: K1, k2tog, ssk, k1. (4 sts)

Row 12: P.

Row 13: K2tog, ssk. (2 sts)

Row 14: P2tog. (1 st)

Break yarn and pull through rem st.

Earflaps

(*make 2*)

With RS facing and using US 9 (5.5 mm) needles and a doubled strand of A, pick up and k 12(14) sts along cast-on edge for first earflap.

Row 1: K2, p8(10), k2.
Row 2: K.
Row 3: K2, p8(10), k2.
Rep Rows 2–3 three times more.
Row 10: K2, k2tog, k to last 4 sts, ssk, k2. (10/12 sts)
Row 11: K2, p to last 2 sts, k2.
Row 12: K.
Row 13: K2, p to last 2 sts, k2.
Rep Rows 10–13 once more. (8/10 sts)
Large size only:
Row 18: K2, k2tog, k2, ssk, k2. (8 sts)
Row 19: K2, p4, k2.
Both sizes:
Next row: K2, k2tog, ssk, k2. (6 sts)
Next row: K2, p2, k2.
Next row: K.
Next row: K2, p2, k2.
Next row: K1, k2tog, ssk, k1. (4 sts)
K 3 rows.
Next row: K2tog, ssk. (2 sts)
K 3 rows.
Next row: K2tog. (1 st)
Break yarn and pull through rem st.
Work second earflap on other side of hat.

Nose

(*make 1*)

Using US 3 (3.25 mm) needles and C, cast on 10 sts.
Work 2 rows in st st beg with a k row.
Row 3: K2tog, k6, ssk. (8 sts)
Row 4: P2tog, p4, p2tog. (6 sts)
Row 5: K2tog, k2, ssk. (4 sts)
Row 6: [P2tog] twice. (2 sts)
Row 7: K2tog. (1 st)
Break yarn and pull through rem st.

Making up and finishing

For general information on putting your hat together, see pages 104–107.

Join back seam of hat using the flat-seam technique (see page 104).

Place one A and one B ear piece RS together. Oversew round two sides then turn ear RS out. Oversew lower edge. Make second ear in the same way. Stitch ears in position.

Using C, embroider a coil of chain stitch (see page 106) for each eye. Using C, embroider an arc of chain stitch across top part of each eye.

Oversew the nose in place. Using C, work a line of chain stitch from nose to garter stitch border of hat.

blizzard the reindeer

When it's snowy outside and you need to keep your head warm, there's nothing cozier—or frankly more suitable—than a knitted reindeer hat topped with a couple of perky antlers. If you want to stand out from the crowd, knit him with a red nose like we've done here. Or for something a little more subtle, knit his nose in black or dark brown. Remember, reindeers are not just for Christmas.

Yarn
2 x 1¾ oz (50 g) balls—each approx 126 yds (115 m) —Rowan Cashsoft DK in shade 517 Donkey (A)
1 x 1¾ oz (50 g) ball—approx 120 yds (110 m)—Debbie Bliss Cashmerino DK in shade 43 Beige (B)
Small amount of Debbie Bliss Rialto DK in shade 12 Red (C)
Small amounts of Sirdar Country Style DK in shade 417 Black (D) and shade 411 Cream (E)
Small amount of fiberfill toy stuffing

You will also need
Sizes US 9 (5.5 mm) and US 3 (3.25 mm) knitting needles
Size US 7 (4.5 mm) crochet hook
Yarn sewing needle
Large-eyed embroidery needle
2 small safety pins

Sizes
3-10 years (11 years and over)

Actual measurements
Approx 17½ in/44 cm (19 in/48 cm) circumference

Gauge (tension)
15 sts and 24 rows to 4 in (10 cm) square over stockinette (stocking) stitch using yarn double on US 9 (5.5 mm) needles.

Main hat
(*make 1*)
Using US 9 (5.5 mm) needles and A, cast on 66(72) sts using yarn double.
Place a small safety pin marker at 22nd(24th) st in from each edge.
Work 22(26) rows in st st beg with a k row.
Large size only:
Row 27: K5, [k2tog, k10] 5 times, k2tog, k5. (66 sts)
Row 28: P.
Both sizes:
Next row: K4, [sl1, k2tog, psso, k8] 5 times, sl1, k2tog, psso, k4. (54 sts)
Next and every WS row until stated otherwise: P.
Next RS row: K3, [sl1, k2tog, psso, k6] 5 times, sl1, k2tog, psso, k3. (42 sts)
Next RS row: K2, [sl1, k2tog, psso, k4] 5 times, sl1, k2tog, psso, k2. (30 sts)
Next RS row: K1, [sl1, k2tog, psso, k2] 5 times, sl1, k2tog, psso, k1. (18 sts)
Next row (WS): [P2tog] to end. (9 sts)
Break yarn leaving a long tail.
Thread yarn tail through rem sts, pull up tightly and secure.

With RS of work facing and using doubled strand of A, pick up and k 22(24) sts across lower edge from RH edge toward first safety pin marker.
Work 3 rows in st st beg with a p row.
Next row: K to last 2 sts, ssk. (21/23 sts)
Next row: P2tog, P to end. (20/22 sts)
Rep last 2 rows 2(3) times more. (16 sts)
Bind (cast) off.

With RS of work facing and using doubled strand of A, pick up and k 22(24) sts across lower edge from second safety pin marker to LH edge.
Work 3 rows in st st beg with a p row.
Next row: K2tog, k to end. (21/23 sts)
Next row: P to last 2 sts, p2tog. (20/22 sts)
Rep last 2 rows twice (3 times) more. (16 sts)
Bind (cast) off.

Ears

(make 4 pieces)

Using US 9 (5.5 mm) needles and A, cast on 10 sts using yarn double.

Work 8 rows in st st beg with a k row.

Row 9: K1, k2tog, k to last 3 sts, ssk, k1. (8 sts)

Row 10: P.

Rep Rows 9-10 once more. (6 sts)

Row 13: K1, k2tog, ssk, k1. (4 sts)

Row 14: [P2tog] twice. (2 sts)

Row 15: K2tog. (1 st)

Break yarn and pull through rem st.

Antlers

(make 4 pieces)

Using US 3 (3.25 mm) needles and B, cast on 5 sts.

Work 8 rows in st st beg with a k row.

Row 9: Inc1, k2, inc1, k1. (7 sts)

Row 10: Inc1 pwise, p to last 2 sts, inc1 pwise, p1. (9 sts)

Row 11: Inc1, k to last 2 sts, inc1, k1. (11 sts)

Row 12: P.

Row 13: K4, M1, k3, M1, k4. (13 sts)

Row 14: P4. Turn and work on these 4 sts only, leaving rem sts on needle.

Work 2 rows in st st beg with a k row.

Row 17: K2tog, ssk. (2 sts)

Row 18: P2tog. (1 st)

Break yarn and pull through rem st.

Rejoin yarn to rem sts on WS of work.

Next row: P5, turn and work on these 5 sts only, leaving rem sts on needle.

Work 5 rows in st st beg with a k row.

Next row: P2tog, p1, p2tog. (3 sts)

Next row: Sl1, k2tog, psso. (1 st)

Break yarn and pull through rem st.

Rejoin yarn to rem 4 sts on WS of work.

Work 3 rows in st st beg with a p row.

Next row: K2tog, ssk. (2 sts)

Next row: P2tog. (1 st)

Break yarn and pull through rem st.

Nose

(make 1)

Using US 3 (3.25 mm) needles and C, cast on 8 sts.

Row 1: Inc1, k to last 2 sts, inc1, k1. (10 sts)

Row 2: Inc1 pwise, p to last 2 sts, inc1pwise, p1. (12 sts)

Row 3: Inc1, k to last 2 sts, inc1, k1. (14 sts)

Work 3 rows in st st beg with a p row.

Row 7: K1, k2tog, k to last 3 sts, ssk, k1. (12 sts)

Row 8: P2tog, p to last 2 sts, p2tog. (10 sts)

Row 9: K1, k2tog, k to last 3 sts, ssk, k1. (8 sts)

Bind (cast) off pwise.

Making up and finishing

For general information on putting your hat together, see pages 104-107.

Join back seam of hat using the flat-seam technique (see page 104).

Place two ear pieces RS together. Oversew sides. Turn ear RS out and oversew lower edge. Make second ear in the same way. Fold ears in half lengthwise and stitch in place along short folded edge, so folded edge is parallel to lower edge of main hat.

Place two antler pieces RS together. Oversew around edges leaving lower edge open for turning and stuffing. Turn antler RS out and stuff very lightly. Make second antler the same way. Stitch antlers in position.

Using D, embroider a small coil of chain stitch (see page 106) for each eye center. Using E, embroider a coil of chain stitch round each eye center.

Oversew nose in place.

Using the crochet hook and a single strand of B, work a crochet edging (see page 107) around entire lower edge of hat, beginning and ending at back seam.

scorch the dragon

More cute than fearsome, this dragon-style balaclava will ward off the chills on even the coldest days. And even if it isn't that cold the hat will be a welcome addition to any boy's stash of dressing-up clothes, particularly if there's a knight around who's getting a bit too big for his boots. Knitted in a soft double-knitting yarn in two coordinating shades of green, this hat comes complete with specially designed pointed spikes and ears.

Yarn
1 x 1¾ oz (50 g) ball–approx 126 yds (115 m)–Rowan Cashsoft DK in shade 541 Spruce (A)
1 x 1¾ oz (50 g) ball–approx 136 yds (125 m)–Rowan Pure Wool DK in shade 19 Avocado (B)
Small amount of fiberfill toy stuffing

You will also need
Size US 5 (3.75 mm) knitting needles
Yarn sewing needle
Large-eyed embroidery needle
Two stitch holders or large safety pins

Size
3–10 years

Actual measurements
Approx 10 in (25 cm) neck circumference, 11 in (28 cm) height

Gauge (tension)
23 sts and 30 rows to 4 in (10 cm) square over stockinette (stocking) stitch using US 5 (3.75 mm) needles.

Main hat
(*make 1*)
Using size US 5 (3.75 mm) needles and A, cast on 70 sts loosely.
Row 1: [K2, p2] to last 2 sts, k2.
Row 2: [P2, k2] to last 2 sts, p2.
Rep first 2 rows 9 times more.
Row 21: [K2, p2] 14 times, k2, leave rem 12 sts on st holder or large safety pin. (58 sts on needle)
Row 22: [P2, k2] 11 times, p2, leave rem 12 sts on st holder or large safety pin. (46 sts on needle)
Row 23: [K3, M1] 7 times, k4, [M1, k3] 7 times. (60 sts)
Row 24: P.
Break A and join in B.
Work 42 rows in st st beg with a k row.
Row 67: K3, M1, k to last 3 sts, M1, k3. (62 sts)
Work 3 rows in st st beg with a k row.
Rep Rows 67–70 once more. (64 sts)
Row 75: K42, sl1, k1, psso, turn.
Row 76: P21, p2tog, turn.
Row 77: K21, sl1, k1, psso, turn.
Rep last 2 rows 17 times more.
Row 112: P21, p2tog, turn.
Row 113: K4, k2tog, k10, ssk, k3, sl1, k1, psso, turn.
Row 114: P21, p2tog, turn.
Row 115: K4, k2tog, k8, ssk, k3, sl1, k1, psso.
Row 116: P to last 2 sts, p2tog. (18 sts)
Break yarn and leave sts on needle.
With RS facing and using A, [k2, p2] 3 times into 12 sts on right st holder, pick up and k 34 sts evenly up right side of hat, k 18 sts from needle, pick up and k 34 sts evenly down left side of hat, [p2, k2] 3 times into 12 sts from left st holder. (110 sts)
Next row: [P2, k2] to last 2 sts, p2.

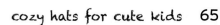

Next row: [K2, p2] to last 2 sts, k2.
Rep last 2 rows twice more.
Bind (cast) off, keeping to the k2, p2 rib pattern.

Spikes
Small spike
(*make 2 pieces*)
Using US 5 (3.75 mm) needles and A, cast on 16 sts.
Work 2 rows in st st beg with a k row.
Row 3: K1, k2tog, k to last 3 sts, ssk, k1. (14 sts)
Row 4: P.
Rep Rows 3-4 four times more. (6 sts)
Row 13: K1, k2tog, ssk, k1. (4 sts)
Row 14: [P2tog] twice. (2 sts)
Row 15: K2tog. (1 st)
Break yarn and pull through rem st.

Medium spike
(*make 2 pieces*)
Using US 5 (3.75 mm) needles and A, cast on 20 sts.
Work 2 rows in st st beg with a k row.
Row 3: K1, k2tog, k to last 3 sts, ssk, k1. (18 sts)
Row 4: P.
Rep Rows 3-4 six times more. (6 sts)
Row 17: K1, k2tog, ssk, k1. (4 sts)
Row 18: [P2tog] twice. (2 sts)
Row 19: K2tog. (1 st)
Break yarn and pull through rem st.

Large spike
(*make 2 pieces*)
Using US 5 (3.75 mm) needles and A, cast on 24 sts.
Work 2 rows in st st beg with a k row.
Row 3: K1, k2tog, k to last 3 sts, ssk, k1. (22 sts)
Row 4: P.
Rep Rows 3-4 eight times more. (6 sts)
Row 21: K1, k2tog, ssk, k1. (4 sts)
Row 22: [P2tog] twice. (2 sts)
Row 23: K2tog. (1 st)
Break yarn and pull through rem st.

Ears
(*make 2*)
Using US 5 (3.75 mm) needles and A, cast on 24 sts.
Work 8 rows in st st beg with a k row.
Row 9: K2, k2tog, k4, ssk, k4, k2tog, k4, ssk, k2. (20 sts)
Row 10 and every WS row until stated otherwise: P.

Row 11 (RS): K2, k2tog, k2, ssk, k4, k2tog, k2, ssk, k2. (16 sts)
Row 13 (RS): K2, k2tog, ssk, k4, k2tog, ssk, k2. (12 sts)
Row 15 (RS): K1, k2tog, ssk, k2, k2tog, ssk, k1. (8 sts)
Row 17 (RS): K1, k2tog, k2, ssk, k1. (6 sts)
Row 19 (RS): K1, k2tog, ssk, k1. (4 sts)
Row 21 (RS): K2tog, ssk. (2 sts)
Row 22 (WS): P2tog. (1 st)
Break yarn and pull through rem st.

Making up and finishing
For general information on putting your hat together, see pages 104-107.

Join front seam at neck using the flat-seam technique (see page 104).

Place two pieces for each spike together with RS facing outwards. Oversew two sides on each, leaving bottom edges open. Stuff spikes very lightly and then oversew lower edge. Oversew spikes in place along center back of head, so largest spike is at base by ribbed border, medium size is immediately above and smallest is at top.

Fold ear pieces in half widthwise so RS face outward. Oversew side seams. Oversew lower seam so that back seam runs down center of ear. Stitch ears in place at top of hat so seams are uppermost and points of ears face inward; ears will then flop downward so seam is on underside.

bamboo the panda

These shy, bamboo-guzzling creatures from China are one of the most striking animals on Earth. Now you can do your bit to help increase the population of these endangered giants by knitting your own! Super simple to knit in just black and white, you can conjure up this cute panda-cub hat in little more than a rainy afternoon.

Yarn

1 x 1¾ oz (50 g) ball–approx 127 yds (116 m)– Sublime Extra Fine Merino DK in shade 13 Jet Black (A)

1(2) x 1¾ oz (50 g) ball(s)–each approx 98 yds (90 m)–Patons Fairytale DK in shade 51 White (B)

You will also need

Sizes US 9 (5.5 mm) and US 3 (3.25 mm) knitting needles
Yarn sewing needle
Large-eyed embroidery needle

Sizes

3–10 years (11 years and over)

Actual measurements

Approx 16 in/41 cm (19½ in/49 cm) circumference

Gauge (tension)

16 sts and 21 rows to 4 in (10 cm) square over stockinette (stocking) stitch using yarn double on US 9 (5.5 mm) needles.

Main hat

(*make 1*)

Using US 9 (5.5 mm) needles and A, cast on 66(78) sts using yarn double.
Row 1: [K2, p2] to last 2 sts, k2.
Row 2: [P2, k2] to last 2 sts, p2.
Rep Rows 1–2 once more.
Break A and join in B, using yarn double.
Work 24(28) rows in st st beg with a k row.
Large size only:
Row 33: K5, [sl1, k2tog, psso, k10] 5 times, sl1, k2tog, psso, k5. (66 sts)
Row 34: P.
Both sizes:
Next row: K4, [sl1, k2tog, psso, k8] 5 times, sl1, k2tog, psso, k4. (54 sts)
Next and every WS row until stated otherwise: P.
Next RS row: K3, [sl1, k2tog, psso, k6] 5 times, sl1, k2tog, psso, k3. (42 sts)
Next RS row: K2, [sl1, k2tog, psso, k4] 5 times, sl1, k2tog, psso, k2. (30 sts)
Next RS row: K1, [sl1, k2tog, psso, k2] 5 times, sl1, k2tog, psso, k1. (18 sts)
Next row (WS): [P2tog] to end. (9 sts)
Break yarn leaving a long tail.
Thread yarn tail through rem sts, pull up tightly and secure.

Ears

(*make 2*)

Using US 9 (5.5 mm) needles and A, cast on 10 sts using yarn double.
Work 6 rows in st st beg with a k row.
Row 7: K2tog, k6, ssk. (8 sts)
Row 8: P2tog, p4, p2tog. (6 sts)
Row 9: K2tog, k2, ssk. (4 sts)
Row 10: [P2tog] twice. (2 sts)
Row 11: [Inc1] twice. (4 sts)
Row 12: [Inc1 pwise, p1] twice. (6 sts)
Row 13: Inc1, k3, inc1, k1. (8 sts)
Row 14: Inc1 pwise, p5, inc1 pwise, p1. (10 sts)
Work 6 rows in st st beg with a k row.
Bind (cast) off.

Eye patches
(*make 2*)

Using US 3 (3.25 mm) needles and A, cast on 6 sts.
Row 1: Inc1, k to last 2 sts, inc1, k1. (8 sts)
Row 2: Inc1 pwise, p to last 2 sts, inc1 pwise, p1. (10 sts)
Rep Rows 1–2 once more. (14 sts)
Work 6 rows in st st beg with a k row.
Row 11: K2tog, k to last 2 sts, ssk. (12 sts)
Row 12: P2tog, p to last 2 sts, p2tog. (10 sts)
Rep Rows 11–12 once more. (6 sts)
Bind (cast) off.

Making up and finishing
For general information on putting your hat together, see pages 104–107.

Join back seam of hat using the flat-seam technique (see page 104).

Fold ear pieces in half widthwise RS together so cast-on and bound- (cast-) off edges meet. Oversew around curved edges then turn ears RS out. Oversew lower edges. Stitch ears in place.

Oversew eye patches in place so they slope slightly downward toward sides of hat.

Using B, embroider a coil of chain stitch (see page 106) for each eye, leaving center of eyes in A.

Using A, embroider a coil of chain stitch in a triangle shape for nose. Using A, work a row of chain stitch from nose to top of ribbed border of hat.

Chapter 3

cool hats for the young at heart

ozzie the koala 72

slinky cat 74

slinky cat mittens 77

kitty the tiger 78

kitty the tiger boot toppers 80

hunter the hound 81

pattie the cow 84

pattie the cow ankle warmers 87

curly the pig 88

frosty the polar bear 90

ozzie the koala

This is the perfect hat for anyone you may know who loves climbing eucalyptus trees and nibbling their leaves. If you don't know anyone in this category, you could always knit it for someone who has fallen in love with these big-nosed, beady-eyed marsupials—or any fan or inhabitant of the land Down Under.

Yarn
2 x 1¾ oz (50 g) balls—each approx 109 yds (100 m)— Katia Maxi Merino in shade 12 Gray (A)
Small amount of Wendy Osprey in shade 2681 Cream (B)
Small amount of Sirdar Country Style DK in shade 417 Black (C)

You will also need
Sizes US 9 (5.5 mm) and US 3 (3.25 mm) knitting needles
Yarn sewing needle
Large-eyed embroidery needle
2 small safety pins
Small nylon brush, such as a nailbrush

Sizes
3-10 years (11 years and over)

Actual measurements
Approx 16 in/41 cm (19½ in/49 cm) circumference

Gauge (tension)
16 sts and 22 rows to 4 in (10 cm) square over stockinette (stocking) stitch using US 9 (5.5 mm) needles.

Main hat
(*make 1*)
Using US 9 (5.5 mm) needles and A, cast on 66(78) sts.
Row 1: [K2, p2] to last 2 sts, k2.
Row 2: [P2, k2] to last 2 sts, p2.
Rep Rows 1-2 once more.
Work 24(28) rows in st st beg with a k row.
Large size only:
Row 33: K5, [sl1, k2tog, psso, k10] 5 times, sl1, k2tog, psso, k5. (66 sts)
Row 34: P.
Both sizes:
Next row: K4, [sl1, k2tog, psso, k8] 5 times, sl1, k2tog, psso, k4. (54 sts)
Next and every WS row: P.
Next RS row: K3, [sl1, k2tog, psso, k6] 5 times, sl1, k2tog, psso, k3. (42 sts)
Next RS row: K2, [sl1, k2tog, psso, k4] 5 times, sl1, k2tog, psso, k2. (30 sts)
Next RS row: K1, [sl1, k2tog, psso, k2] 5 times, sl1, k2tog, psso, k1. (18 sts)
Bind (cast) off kwise on WS of work.

Ears
(*make 4 pieces*)
Using US 9 (5.5 mm) needles and A, cast on 12 sts.
Work 4 rows in st st beg with a k row.
Break A and join in B, using yarn double.
Work 4 rows in st st beg with a k row.
Row 9: K1, k2tog, k to last 3 sts, ssk, k1. (10 sts)
Row 10: P2tog, p to last 2 sts, p2tog. (8 sts)
Bind (cast) off.

Earflaps
(*make 2*)
With RS facing and using US 9 (5.5 mm) needles and A, pick up and k12(14) sts along the cast-on edge for the first earflap.
Row 1: K2, p to last 2 sts, k2.
Row 2: K.
Row 3: K2, p to last 2 sts, k2.
Rep Rows 2-3 twice(once) more.
Next row: K2, k2tog, k4(6), ssk, k2. (10/12 sts)
Next row: K2, p to last 2 sts, k2.
Next row: K2, k2tog, k2(4), ssk, k2. (8/10 sts)

Next row: K2, p to last 2 sts, k2.
Large size only:
Next row: K2, k2tog, k2, ssk, k2. (8 sts)
Next row: K2, p to last 2 sts, k2.
Both sizes:
Next row: K2, k2tog, ssk, k2. (6 sts)
Next row: K2tog, k2, ssk. (4 sts)
Next row: K2tog, ssk. (2 sts)
Next row: K2tog. (1 st)
Break yarn and pull through rem st.
Work second earflap in the same way.

Nose
Using US 3 (3.25 mm) needles and C, cast on 8 sts.
Row 1: Inc1, k to last 2 sts, inc1, k1. (10 sts)
Row 2: P.
Rep Rows 1–2 twice more. (14 sts)
Work 8 rows in st st beg with a k row.
Row 15: K2tog, k to last 2 sts, ssk. (12 sts)
Row 16: P.
Rep Rows 15–16 once more. (10 sts)
Row 19: K2tog, k to last 2 sts, ssk. (8 sts)
Bind (cast) off kwise on WS of work.

Making up and finishing
For general information on putting your hat together, see pages 104–107.

Join back of hat using the flat-seam technique (see page 104).

Place two ear pieces RS together. Oversew sides, leaving lower edge open, then turn ear RS out. Oversew lower edge. Make second ear in the same way. Stitch ears in place. To give ears a characteristic fuzzy look, dampen and brush quite vigorously with the nylon brush.

Oversew nose in place.

Using C, embroider a coil of chain stitch (see page 106) for each eye.

Tip

Before picking up stitches for the earflaps, fold the main hat piece together, so the two short ends meet at the center. Place a small safety pin at each side of the hat at the cast-on edge to mark the center of each earflap. Pick up an equal number of stitches on either side of the marker for each earflap.

slinky cat

Velvety, soft, and feminine... the three best words to describe this knitted kitty hat. Worked in a beautiful super-chunky alpaca yarn in rich gray, this gorgeous feline has slanting eyes and a slightly superior air. Knit one for a kitty-owning friend in colors that match her own pet. The hat is designed to sit fairly high up on the head, but if you would like something a little longer, simply add a few rows when you're knitting the main part of the hat.

Yarn
2 x 1¾ oz (50 g) balls—each approx 75 yds (80 m)—
    Wendy Norse Chunky shade 2701 Porpoise (A)
1¾ oz (50 g) ball—approx 113 yds (112 m)—King Cole
    Merino Blend DK in shade 857 Bark (B)
Small amounts of Sirdar Country Style DK in shade
    411 Cream (C), shade 417 Black (D) and shade 434
    Silver Cloud (E)

You will also need
Sizes US 9 (5.5 mm), US 10.5 (6.5 mm), and US 3
    (3.25 mm) knitting needles
Yarn sewing needle
Large-eyed embroidery needle

Sizes
5-10 years (11 years and over)

Actual measurements
Approx 18 in/46 cm (21 in/53 cm) circumference

Gauge (tension)
16 sts and 20 rows to 4 in (10 cm) square over
    stockinette (stocking) stitch using US 10.5
    (6.5 mm) needles.

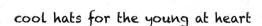

Main hat
(*make 1*)
Using US 9 (5.5 mm) needles and A, cast on 72(82) sts.
Large size only:
Row 1: [K2, p2] to last 2 sts, k2.
Row 2: [P2, k2] to last 2 sts, p2.
Rep Rows 1-2 once more.
Small size only:
Row 1: [K2, p2] to end.
Rep last row 3 times more.
Change to size US 10.5 (6.5 mm) needles.
Work 16(14) rows in st st beg with a k row.
Large size only:
Next row: K4, [ssk, k6] 5 times, [k2tog, k6] 4 times, k2tog, k4. (72 sts)
Work 3 rows in st st beg with a p row.
Both sizes:
Next row: K3, [sl1, k2tog, psso, k4] 9 times, sl1, k2tog, psso, k3. (52 sts)
Work 3 rows in st st beg with a p row.
Next row: K2, [sl1, k2tog, psso, k2] 9 times, sl1, k2tog, psso, k2. (32 sts)
Work 3 rows in st st beg with a p row.
Next row: K1, [sl1, k2tog, psso] 10 times, k1. (12 sts)
Break yarn leaving a long tail.
Thread yarn tail through rem sts, pull up tightly and secure.

Ears
(*make 2 in A and 2 in B*)
Using US 10.5 (6.5 mm) needles and with treble strands of yarn for B, cast on 10 sts.
Work 2 rows in st st beg with a k row.
Row 3: K1, k2tog, k to last 3 sts, ssk, k1. (8 sts)
Row 4: P.
Rep Rows 3-4 once more. (6 sts)
Row 7: K1, k2tog, ssk, k1. (4 sts)
Row 8: [P2tog] twice. (2 sts)
Row 9: K2tog. (1 st)
Break yarn and pull through rem st.

Outer eyes
(*make 2*)
The eyes are worked from the inside of the eye outward.
Using US 3 (3.25 mm) needles and C, cast on 2 sts.
Row 1: [Inc1] twice. (4 sts)
Row 2: P.

Row 3: Inc1, k to last 2 sts, inc1, k1. (6 sts)
Row 4: P.
Rep Rows 3-4 once more. (8 sts)
Work 6 rows in st st beg with a k row.
Row 13: K2tog, k to last 2 sts, ssk. (6 sts)
Row 14: P.
Rep Rows 13-14 once more. (4 sts)
Row 17: K2tog, ssk. (2 sts)
Row 18: P2tog. (1 st)
Break yarn and pull through rem st.

Nose
(*make 1*)
Using US 3 (3.25 mm) needles and D, cast on 10 sts.
Work 2 rows in st st beg with a k row.
Row 3: K2tog, k to last 2 sts, ssk. (8 sts)
Row 4: P.
Rep Rows 3-4 twice more. (4 sts)
Row 7: K2tog, ssk. (2 sts)
Row 8: P2tog. (1 st)
Break yarn and pull through rem st.

Making up and finishing
For general information on putting your hat together, see pages 104-107.

Join the back seam of the hat using the flat-seam technique (see page 104).

Place one A and one B ear piece RS together. Oversew side seams using A, then turn ear RS out. Oversew lower edge. Make second ear the same way. Stitch ears in place.

Oversew outer eyes in place, remembering to slant eyes slightly as shown in the photograph. Using D, embroider a coil of chain stitch (see page 106) for each eye center, and four straight stitches above each eye for eyelashes.

Oversew nose in place. Using D double, work a line of chain stitch from the nose to the ribbed border of the hat. Using E, embroider whiskers in stem stitch (see page 106).

slinky cat mittens

Knitted in a beautiful shade of deep gray, these warm fingerless mittens co-ordinate perfectly with the paler gray cat hat on page 74. They will keep your hands as warm as toast, even on the chilliest winter days.

Yarn
1 x 3½ oz (100 g) ball–approx 87 yds (80 m)–Rowan Big Wool in shade 7 Smoky (A)
1 x 3½ oz (100 g)–approx 262 yds (240 m)–Katia Merino Blend DK in shade 25 Pale Pink (B)

You will also need
Sizes US 10.5 (6.5 mm) and US 3 (3.25 mm) knitting needles
Stitch holder
Yarn sewing needle
Large-eyed embroidery needle

Sizes
7-10 years (11 years and over)

Actual measurements
Approx 3 in/8 cm (4 in/10 cm) width laid flat

Gauge (tension)
11 sts and 16 rows to 4 in (10 cm) square over stockinette (stocking) stitch using US 10.5 (6.5 mm) needles.

Mitten
(*make 2*)
Using US 10.5 (6.5 mm) needles and A, cast on 18 (22) sts.
Row 1: [K2, p2] to last 2 sts, k2.
Row 2: [P2, k2] to last 2 sts, p2.
Rep first 2 rows 4(5) times more.
Work 6(8) rows in st st beg with a k row.
Next row: K8(9), M1, k2(4), M1, k8(9). (20/24 sts)

Next and every WS row: P.
Next RS row: K8(9), M1, k4(6), M1, k8(9). (22/26 sts)
Next RS row: K8(9), M1, k6(8), M1, k8(9). (24/28 sts)
Next RS row: K8(9), break yarn, put next 8(10) sts on stitch holder, rejoin yarn, k8(9). (16/18 sts)
Work 3(5) rows in st st beg with a p row.
Next row: P.
Bind (cast) off kwise.

Put 10 sts from holder onto US 10.5 (6.5 mm) needle.
Work 3 rows in st st beg with a k row.
Bind (cast) off pwise.

Paws
Main pad
(*make 2*)
Using US 3 (3.25 mm) needles and B, cast on 16 sts.
Work 6 rows in st st beg with a k row.
Row 7: K2tog, k to last 2 sts, ssk. (14 sts)
Row 8: P.
Rep Rows 7-8 three times more. (8 sts)
Row 15: K2tog, k to last 2 sts, ssk. (6 sts)
Bind (cast) off kwise on WS of work.

Small pads
(*make 6*)
Using US 3 (3.25 mm) needles and B, cast on 4 sts.
Row 1: Inc1, k1, inc1, k1. (6 sts)
Row 2: P.
Row 3: K2tog, k2, ssk. (4 sts)
Row 4: [P2tog] twice. (2 sts)
Row 5: K2tog. (1 st)
Break yarn and pull through rem st.

Making up and finishing
Join side seams of mittens and thumbs using the flat-seam technique (see page 104).

Oversew paw pads in place, remembering that thumb should be on right of one mitten and on left of other mitten.

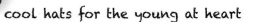

kitty the tiger

In this cutely striped head gear, you will have to provide the tiger-like snarl and growl for yourself. The hat has cozy easy-to-knit earflaps for added warmth and style—though you can omit these if you want a slightly simpler look. The main part of the hat is knitted using two strands of standard DK yarn in black and a gorgeous shade of burnt orange.

Yarn
2 x 1³/₄ oz (50 g) balls—each approx 164 yds (150 m)—Click Sirdar DK in shade 188 Rustica (A)
1 x 1³/₄ oz (50 g) ball—approx 164 yds (150 m)—Click Sirdar DK in shade 138 Black (B)
Small amount of Sirdar Country Style DK in shade 411 Cream (C)

You will also need
Sizes US 9 (5.5 mm) and US 3 (3.25 mm) knitting needles
Yarn sewing needle
Large-eyed embroidery needle
2 small safety pins

Sizes
3-10 years (11 years and over)

Actual measurements
Approx 16 in/41 cm (19½ in/ 49 cm) circumference

Gauge (tension)
16 sts and 22 rows to 4 in (10 cm) square over stockinette (stocking) stitch using yarn double on US 9 (5.5 mm) needles.

Main hat
(make 1)
Using US 9 (5.5 mm) needles and A, cast on 66(78) sts using yarn double.
K 4 rows.
Work 4 rows in st st beg with a k row.
Break A and join in B, using yarn double.
Row 9: K26(32) in B, rejoin A, k14 in A, k in B to end.
Row 10: P26(32) in B, p14 in A, p in B to end.
Work 2 rows st st in A, beg with a k row.
Row 13: K29(35) in B, k8 in A, k in B to end.
Row 14: P29(35) in B, p8 in A, p in B to end.
Work 2 rows st st in A, beg with a k row.
Row 17: K26(32) in B, k14 in A, k in B to end.
Row 18: P26(32) in B, p14 in A, p in B to end.
Cont in A only, break yarn no longer in use.
Work 6(8) rows in st st beg with a k row.
Large size only:

Row 27: K5, [sl1, k2tog, psso, k10] 5 times, sl1, k2tog, psso, k5. (66 sts)
Work 3 rows in st st beg with a p row.
Both sizes:
Next row: K4, [sl1, k2tog, psso, k8] 5 times, sl1, k2tog, psso, k4. (54 sts)
Work 3 rows in st st beg with a p row.
Next row: K3, [sl1, k2tog, psso, k6] 5 times, sl1, k2tog, psso, k3. (42 sts)
Work 3 rows in st st beg with a p row.
Next row: K2, [sl1, k2tog, psso, k4] 5 times, sl1, k2tog, psso, k2. (30 sts)
Work 3 rows in st st beg with a p row.
Bind (cast) off.

Before picking up stitches for the earflaps, fold the main hat piece together, so the two short ends meet at the center. Place a small safety pin at each side of the hat at the cast-on edge to mark the center of each earflap. Pick up an equal number of stitches on either side of the marker for each earflap.

Tip

Earflaps
(*make 2*)
With RS facing and using US 9 (5.5 mm) needles and a doubled strand of A, pick up and k 12(14) sts along cast-on edge for first earflap.
Row 1: K2, p to last 2 sts, k2.
Row 2: K.
Rep Rows 1-2 twice(once) more.
Next and every WS row until stated otherwise: K2, p to last 2 sts, k2.
Large size only:
Next RS row: K2, k2tog, k to last 4 sts, ssk, k2. (12 sts)
Both sizes:
Next RS row: K.
Next RS row: K2, k2tog, k to last 4 sts, ssk, k2. (10 sts)
Next RS row: K2, k2tog, k to last 4 sts, ssk, k2. (8 sts)
Next row (WS): K.
Next row: K2tog, k4, ssk. (6 sts)
Next row: K2tog, k2, ssk. (4 sts)
Bind (cast) off pwise.
Work second earflap in the same way.

Ears
(*make 4 pieces*)
Using US 9 (5.5 mm) needles and A, cast on 10 sts using yarn double.
Work 6 rows in st st beg with a k row.
Row 7: K1, k2tog, k4, ssk, k1. (8 sts)
Row 8: P.
Row 9: K1, k2tog, k2, ssk, k1. (6 sts)
Row 10: P2tog, p2, p2tog. (4 sts)
Row 11: K2tog, ssk. (2 sts)
Row 12: P2tog. (1 st)
Break yarn and pull through rem st.

Outer eyes
(*make 2*)
Using US 3 (3.25 mm) needles and C, cast on 5 sts.
Row 1: Inc1, k to last 2 sts, inc1, k1. (7 sts)
Row 2: P.
Rep Rows 1-2 three times more. (13 sts)
Row 9: K1, k2tog, k to last 3 sts, ssk, k1. (11 sts)
Row 10: P.
Rep Rows 9-10 twice more. (7 sts)
Row 15: K1, k2tog, k1, ssk, k1. (5 sts)
Bind (cast) off kwise.

Nose
(*make 1*)
Using US 3 (3.25 mm) needles and B, cast on 10 sts.
Row 1: Inc1, k to last 2 sts, inc1, k1. (12 sts)
Row 2: P.
Rep Rows 1-2 once more. (14 sts)
Row 5: K1, k2tog, k to last 3 sts, ssk, k1. (12 sts)
Row 6: P.
Rep Rows 5-6 once more. (10 sts)
Row 9: K1, k2tog, k4, ssk, k1. (8 sts)
Row 10: P2tog, p4, p2tog. (6 sts)
Bind (cast) off.

Making up and finishing
For general information on putting your hat together, see pages 104-107.

Join back seam of hat using the flat-seam technique (see page 104).

Place two ear pieces RS together and oversew round curved edge. Turn RS out and oversew lower edge. Rep for second ear. Stitch ears in place.

Oversew outer eyes in place. Using B, embroider a coil of chain stitch (see page 106) for each eye center.

Oversew nose in place. Using a doubled strand of B, embroider a row of chain stitch from nose to garter stitch border of hat. Using a doubled strand of B, embroider lines at top of head in chain stitch.

kitty the tiger boot toppers

Ggggrrrr..... To keep that winter chill from swirling round your ankles and down into your boots, get out your needles and start knitting yourself these stunning tiger-striped boot toppers. Designed to tuck into the inside of your boots—and add a decorative touch outside—they're the perfect accent for any animal print outfit and a wonderful add-on for the tiger hat on page 78.

Yarn
1 x 1¾ oz (50 g) ball—approx 164 yds (150 m)—Click Sirdar DK in shade 138 Black (A)
1 x 1¾ oz (50 g) ball—approx 164 yds (150 m)—Click Sirdar DK in shade 188 Rustica (B)
Two ¾ in (17 mm) black buttons

You will also need
Sizes US 5 (3.75 mm) and US 3 (3.25 mm) knitting needles
Yarn sewing needle
Large-eyed embroidery needle

Sizes
7–10 years (11 years and over)

Actual measurements
Approx 4½ in/11 cm (5 in/13 cm) width laid flat

Gauge (tension)
23 sts and 30 rows to 4 in (10 cm) square over stockinette (stocking) stitch using US 5 (3.75 mm) needles.

Boot topper
(*make 2*)
Using US 5 (3.75 mm) needles and A, cast on 52(60) sts.
Row 1: K2, p2 to end.
Rep first row 11 times more.
Leave A at side and join in B.
Work 6 rows in st st beg with a k row.
Leave B at side and pick up A.
Work 2 rows in st st beg with a k row.
Rep last 8 rows 4 times more.
Leave A at the side and pick up B.
Work 6 rows in st st beg with a k row.
Break B and cont in A only.
Row 59: K.
Row 60: [K2, p2] to end.
Rep last row 10 times more.
Bind (cast) off keeping to the k2, p2 pattern.

Side tabs
(*make 2*)
Using US 3 (3.25 mm) needles and A, cast on 7 sts.
K 24 rows.
Row 25: K2tog, k3, ssk. (5 sts)
Row 26: K.
Row 27: K2tog, k1, ssk. (3 sts)
Row 28: K.
Row 29: Sl1, k2tog, psso. (1 st)
Break yarn and pull through rem st.

Making up and finishing
Sew seams using mattress stitch (see page 104).

Oversew short straight edges of tabs to middle black stripe of boot topper, opposite seam. Stretch tab down slightly toward lower edge and secure pointed ends with buttons, using a separated strand of A.

Tuck top part of boot topper down into bottom part, so part with tab is on outside.

hunter the hound

With droopy ears and sporting a cute eye patch, this lovable pooch is a perfect personality match for any playful yet hard-to-discipline young teen. He's knitted here in a tweedy brown, but you can knit him in any neutral shade you fancy—to co-ordinate perfectly with your child's favorite outfit or even to match the family pet.

Yarn
2 x 1¾ oz (50 g) balls—each approx 164 yds (150 m) —Sirdar Click DK in shade 120 Bracken (A)
Small amounts of Sirdar Country Style DK in shade 409 Naturelle (B) and shade 417 Black (C)
Small amount of Patons Diploma Gold DK in shade 6184 Steel (D)

You will also need
Sizes US 9 (5.5 mm) and US 3 (3.25 mm) knitting needles
Yarn sewing needle
Large-eyed embroidery needle
2 small safety pins

Sizes
3-10 years (11 years and over)

Actual measurements
Approx 15½ in/39 cm (18 in/46 cm) circumference

Gauge (tension)
17 sts and 21 rows to 4 in (10 cm) square over stockinette (stocking) stitch using yarn double on US 9 (5.5 mm) needles.

Main hat
(*make 1*)
Using US 9 (5.5 mm) needles and A, cast on 66(78) sts using yarn double.
Row 1: [K1, p1] to end.
Row 2: [P1, k1] to end.
Rep Rows 1-2 once more.
Work 26(30) rows in st st beg with a k row.
Large size only:
Row 35: K5, [sl1, k2tog, psso, k10] 5 times, sl1, k2tog, psso, k5. (66 sts)
Row 36: P.
Both sizes:
Next RS row: K4, [sl1, k2tog, psso, k8] 5 times, sl1, k2tog, psso, k4. (54 sts)
Next and every WS row until stated otherwise: P.

Next RS row: K3, [sl1, k2tog, psso, k6] 5 times, sl1, k2tog, psso, k3. (42 sts)
Next RS row: K2, [sl1, k2tog, psso, k4] 5 times, sl1, k2tog, psso, k2. (30 sts)
Next RS row: K1, [sl1, k2tog, psso, k2] 5 times, sl1, k2tog, psso, k1. (18 sts)
Next row (WS): [P2tog] to end. (9 sts)
Break yarn leaving a long tail.
Thread the tail through rem sts, pull tightly and secure.

Earflaps
(*make 2*)
With RS facing and using US 9 (5.5 mm) needles and a doubled strand of A, pick up and k 14(18) sts along the cast-on edge for first earflap.
Row 1: [K1, p1] to end.
Row 2: [P1, k1] to end.
Row 3: [K1, p1] to end.
Row 4: K2tog, [p1, k1] to last 2 sts, p2tog. (12/16 sts)
Row 5: [P1, k1] to end.
Row 6: [K1, p1] to end.
Row 7: [P1, k1] to end.
Row 8: P2tog, [k1, p1] to last 2 sts, k2tog. (10/14 sts)
Row 9: [K1, p1] to end.
Row 10: [P1, k1] to end.
Row 11: [K1, p1] to end.
Rep Rows 4–11 once(twice) more. (6 sts)
Next row: K2tog, p1, k1, p2tog. (4 sts)
Next row: [P1, k1] twice.
Next row: [K1, p1] twice
Next row: [P1, k1] twice.
Next row: P2tog, k2tog. (2 sts)
Next row: K1, p1.
Next row: P1, k1.
Next row: K1, p1.
Next row: K2tog. (1 st)
Break yarn pull through rem st.
Work second earflap in the same way.

Before picking up stitches for the earflaps, fold the main hat piece together, so the two short ends meet at the center. Place a small safety pin at each side of the hat at the cast-on edge to mark the center of each earflap. Pick up an equal number of stitches on either side of the marker for each earflap.

Tip

Ears
(*make 4 pieces*)
Using US 9 (5.5 mm) needles and A, cast on 9 sts using yarn double.
Work 6 rows in st st beg with a k row.
Row 7: Inc1, k to last 2 sts, inc1, k1. (11 sts)
Work 11 rows in st st beg with a p row.
Row 19: K1, k2tog, k5, ssk, k1. (9 sts)
Row 20: P2tog, p5, p2tog. (7 sts)
Bind (cast) off.

Eye patch
(*make 1*)
Using US 3 (3.25 mm) needles and B, cast on 8 sts.
Row 1: Inc1, k to last 2 sts, inc1, k1. (10 sts)
Row 2: P.
Rep Rows 1–2 twice more. (14 sts)
Work 4 rows in st st beg with a k row.
Row 11: K2tog, k to last 2 sts, ssk. (12 sts)
Row 12: P.
Rep last 2 rows once more. (10 sts)
Bind (cast) off.

Making up and finishing

For general information on putting your hat together,
see pages 104–107.

Join back of hat using the flat-seam technique (see
page 104).

Place two ear pieces RS together. Oversew sides, leaving
lower edge open, then turn ear RS out. Oversew lower
edge. Make second ear in the same way. Stitch both ears
in place.

Oversew eye patch in place. Using B yarn, embroider a
circle of chain stitch (see page 106) round outer edge of
patch. Using D, embroider a coil of chain stitch for each
outer eye. Using C, work a French knot (see page 106) in
center of each eye.

Using C, embroider a coil of chain stitch in a flattened oval
shape for nose. Work two straight stitches, one on top of
the other, from lower edge of nose to top of seed (moss)
stitch border of hat.

pattie the cow

With her soft pale pink nose and eyes that will break your heart, this cow is so realistic you can almost hear her moo. We've knitted the cow in contrasting blocks of black and white—and given her one ear in each color—but if you fancy knitting yourself up another breed, just change your colors. And if the fancy takes you, why not knit yourself up a whole herd?

Yarn
2 x 1¾ oz (50 g) balls—each approx 98 yds (90 m)—
 Patons Fairytale Dreamtime DK in shade 51
 White (A)
1 x 1¾ oz (50 g) ball—approx 131 yds (120 m)—Patons
 Diploma Gold DK in shade 6183 Black (B)
Small amount of Katia Merino Blend DK in shade 25
 Pale pink (C)
Small amount of Sirdar Country Style DK in shade
 473 Slate (D)

You will also need
Sizes US 9 (5.5 mm) and US 3 (3.25 mm) knitting
 needles
Size US D-3 (3.25 mm) crochet hook
Yarn sewing needle
Large-eyed embroidery needle

Sizes
3-10 years (11 years and over)

Actual measurements
Approx 16 in/41 cm (19½ in/49 cm) circumference

Gauge (tension)
16 sts and 22 rows to 4 in (10 cm) square over
 stockinette (stocking) stitch using US 9 (5.5 mm)
 needles and yarn double.

Notes
Before you begin knitting, prepare two separate balls of A; Ball 1 consisting of 10 yds (9 m) of doubled yarn and Ball 2 consisting of 1 yd (1 m) of doubled yarn.
 For the hat and ears, use doubled strands of yarn throughout.

Main hat
(*make 1*)
Using US 9 (5.5 mm) needles, cast on 28(33) sts in Ball 1 of A, 12 sts in double strand of C, and 28(33) sts in main ball of A, using yarn double. (68/78 sts)
Row 1: K28(33) in A, k12 in C, k28(33) in A.
Rep first row 3 times more.
Row 5: K28(33) in A, k12 in C, k28(33) in A.
Row 6: P28(33) in A, p12 in C, p28(33) in A.
Row 7: K28(33) in A, k12 in C, k28(33) in A.
Row 8: P28(33) in A, p5 in C, join Ball 2 of A, p2 in A, p5 in C, p28(33) in A.
Row 9: K28(33) in A, k5 in C, k2 in A, k5 in C, k28(33) in A.
Row 10: P27(32) in A, p2tog in A, p4 in C, p2 in A, p4 in C, p2tog in A, p27(32) in A. (66/76 sts)
Using A, work 2 rows in st st beg with a k row.
Join in double strand of B.
Row 13: K21(26) in B, k in A to end.
Row 14: P44(49) in A, p in B to end.
Row 15: K22(27) in B, k in A to end.
Row 16: P44(49) in A, p in B to end.
Row 17: K28(33) in B, k in A to end.
Row 18: P37(42) in A, p in B to end.
Row 19: K29(34) in B, k in A to end.
Row 20: P37(42) in A, p in B to end.
Large size only:
Rep Rows 19-20 once more.
Both sizes:
Next row: K28(33) in B, k in A to end.
Next row: P39(44) in A, p in B to end.
Next row: K26(31) in B, k in A to end.
Next row: P40(45) in A, p in B to end.
Rep last 2 rows 2(3) times more.
Large size only:
Row 33: Using B, k5, [sl1, k2tog, psso, k10] twice; using A, k2tog, k10, ssk, k10, sl1, k2tog, psso, k10, sl1, k2tog, psso, k5. (66 sts)
Row 34: P39 in A, p in B to end.
Both sizes:
Next row: Using B, k4, [sl1, k2tog, psso, k8] twice; using A, [sl1, k2tog, psso, k8] 3 times, sl1, k2tog, psso, k4. (54 sts)
Next row: P36 in A, p in B to end.

Next row: Using B, k3, sl1, k2tog, psso, k6, sl1, k2tog, psso, k3; using A, k3, [sl1, k2tog, psso, k6] 3 times, sl1, k2tog, psso, k3. (42 sts)

Next row: P28 in A, p in B to end.

Next row: Using B, k2, sl1, k2tog, psso, k4, sl1, k2tog, psso, k2; using A, k2, [sl1, k2tog, psso, k4] 3 times, sl1, k2tog, psso, k2. (30 sts)

Next row: P20 in A, p in B to end.

Next row: Using B, k1, sl1, k2tog, psso, k2, sl1, k2tog, psso, k1; using A, k1, [sl1, k2tog, psso, k2] 3 times, sl1, k2tog, psso, k1. (18 sts)

Next row: Using A, [p2tog] 6 times; using B, [p2tog] 3 times. (9 sts)
Break yarn leaving a long tail. Thread the tail through rem sts, pull up tightly and secure.

Ears
(*make 2 pieces in A and 2 pieces in B*)
Using US 9 (5.5 mm) needles and yarn doubled, cast on 4 sts.
Row 1: Inc1, k to last 2 sts, inc1, k1. (6 sts)
Row 2: P.
Rep Rows 1-2 twice more. (10 sts)
Work 4 rows in st st beg with a k row.
Row 11: K1, k2tog, k to last 3 sts, ssk, k1. (8 sts)
Row 12: P.
Rep Rows 11-12 once more. (6 sts)
Row 15: K1, k2tog, ssk, k1. (4 sts)
Row 16: [P2tog] twice.
Row 17: K2tog. (1 st)
Break yarn and pull through rem st.

Outer eyes
(*make 2*)
The eyes are worked from the inside of the eye outwards
Using US 3 (3.25 mm) needles and A, cast on 2 sts.
Row 1: [Inc1] twice. (4 sts)
Row 2: P.
Row 3: Inc1, k1, inc1, k1. (6 sts)
Row 4: P.
Work 6 rows in st st beg with a k row.
Row 11: K2tog, k2, ssk. (4 sts)
Row 12: P.
Row 13: K2tog, ssk. (2 sts)
Row 14: P2tog. (1 st)
Break yarn and pull through rem st.

Making up and finishing
For general information on putting your hat together, see pages 104-107.

Join back seam of hat using the flat-seam technique (see page 104).

Place two B ear pieces RS together and two A ear pieces RS together. Oversew round curved edges using matching yarn. Turn ears RS out. Oversew lower edges. Stitch ears in place.

For curls on top of head, using the crochet hook and A, work a 13 in (33 cm) chain. Arrange chain into three loops and stitch to top of hat, between ears.

Oversew outer eyes in place. Using B, embroider a coil of chain stitch (see page 106) for the center of each eye. Using B, work a line of chain stitch across top of eyes. Using B, embroider three lashes above the left eye in chain stitch.

Using C, outline nose in chain stitch. Using D, work two small circles in chain stitch for nostrils.

pattie the cow
ankle warmers

A draft round your ankles is never a good thing! So why not whip yourself up a pair of these metaphorically cool cow-hide ankle warmers. They are the ideal beginner project if you're just learning to knit a pattern following a chart. For a hat to set your cow ankle warmers off perfectly, turn to page 84.

Yarn
2 x 1¾ oz (50 g) balls—each approx 98 yds (90 m) —Patons Fairytale Dreamtime DK in shade 51 White (A)
1 x 1¾ oz (50 g) ball—approx 131 yds (120 m)—Patons Diploma Gold DK in shade 6183 Black (B)

You will also need
Size US 3 (3.25 mm) knitting needles
Yarn sewing needle

Sizes
7-10 years (11 years and over)

Actual measurements
Approx 4¾ in/12 cm (5½ in/14 cm) width laid flat

Gauge (tension)
22 sts and 26 rows to 4 in (10 cm) square over stockinette (stocking) stitch using US 5 (3.75 mm) needles.

Ankle warmer
(*make 2*)
Using US 3 (3.25 mm) needles and A, cast on 56(60) sts.
Row 1: [K2, p2] to end.
Rep first row 11 times more.
Work 2 rows in st st beg with a k row.
Join in B and follow the chart on page 104 for next 22 rows, working in st st beg with a k row (begin 4 sts in on chart for smaller size).
Break B, cont in A.
Row 37: P.
Row 38: [K2, p2] to end.
Rep last row 11 times more.
Bind (cast) off.

Making up and finishing
Sew seams of ankle warmers using mattress stitch (see page 104).

curly the pig

Knitted in a lovely soft yarn in a perfect shade of piggy pink, this simple hat is the perfect antidote to the winter blues and a must-have for those thousands of pig lovers. It is one of the easiest intermediate patterns in the book—and if you opt for felt rather than embroidered eyes, you can make the project even simpler to complete.

Yarn
1 x 3½ oz (100 g) ball—approx 262 yds (240 m)—
  Katia Merino Blend DK in shade 25 Pale pink (A)
Small amounts of Sirdar Country Style DK in shade
  473 Slate (B) and shade 412 White (C)

You will also need
Sizes US 9 (5.5 mm) and US 6 (4 mm) knitting
  needles
Yarn sewing needle
Large-eyed embroidery needle

Sizes
3-10 years (11 years and over)

Actual measurements
Approx 15½ in/39 cm (18 in/46 cm) circumference

Gauge (tension)
17 sts and 21 rows to 4 in (10 cm) square over
  stockinette (stocking) stitch using yarn double
  on US 9 (5.5 mm) needles.

Main hat
(*make 1*)
Using US 9 (5.5 mm) needles and A, cast on 66(78) sts using yarn double.
Work 30(34) rows in st st beg with a k row.
Large size only:
Row 35: K5, [sl1, k2tog, psso, k10] 5 times, sl1, k2tog, psso, k5. (66 sts)
Row 36: P.
Both sizes:
Next row: K4, [sl1, k2tog, psso, k8] 5 times, sl1, k2tog, psso, k4. (54 sts)
Next and every WS row until stated otherwise: P.
Next RS row: K3, [sl1, k2tog, psso, k6] 5 times, sl1, k2tog, psso, k3. (42 sts)
Next RS row: K2, [sl1, k2tog, psso, k4] 5 times, sl1, k2tog, psso, k2. (30 sts)

Next RS row: K1, [sl1, k2tog, psso, k2] 5 times, sl1, k2tog, psso, k1. (18 sts)
Next row (WS): [P2tog] to end. (9 sts)
Break yarn leaving a long tail.
Thread the tail through rem sts, pull up tightly and secure.

Ears
(*make 2*)
Using US 6 (4 mm) needles and A, cast on 16 sts.
Work 10 rows in st st beg with a k row.
Row 11: K2, k2tog, k to last 4 sts, ssk, k2. (14 sts)
Row 12: P.
Rep Rows 11-12 three times more. (8 sts)
Row 19: K2, k2tog, ssk, k2. (6 sts)
Row 20: P.
Row 21: K1, k2tog, ssk, k1. (4 sts)
Row 22: [P2tog] twice. (2 sts)
Row 23: K2tog. (1 st)
Break yarn and pull through rem st.

Snout
(*make 1*)
Using US 6 (4 mm) needles and A, cast on 10 sts.
Row 1: Inc1, k to last 2 sts, inc1, k1. (12 sts)
Row 2: P.
Rep Rows 1-2 once more. (14 sts)
Row 5: K2, M1, k to last 2 sts, M1, k2. (16 sts)
Row 6: P.

Rep Rows 5-6 once more. (18 sts)
Row 9: K1, k2tog, k to last 3 sts, ssk, k1. (16 sts)
Row 10: P.
Rep Rows 9-10 once more. (14 sts)
Row 13: K1, k2tog, k to last 3 sts, ssk, k1. (12 sts)
Row 14: P2tog, p to last 2 sts, p2tog. (10 sts)
Bind (cast) off.

Making up and finishing
For general information on putting your hat together, see pages 104-107.

Join back seam of hat using the flat-seam technique (see page 104).

Place two ear pieces RS together. Oversew sides, leaving lower edge open. Turn ear RS out and oversew lower edge. Make second ear in the same way. Stitch ears in place.

Oversew snout in place; bound-(cast-)off edge should be lower edge of snout.

Using B, embroider a coil of chain stitch (see page 106) for each eye center. Using C, work a single circle of chain stitch round each eye center.

Using B, work two short rows of chain stitch for nostrils.

frosty the polar bear

What better animal headgear to pull over your ears on an icy day than a polar bear hat? Knitted in beautiful off-white chunky yarn, this hat is so quick to knit, you'll probably want to knit one for every family member. The features are made of simple felt, so this is an ideal project for someone just getting into the swing of knitting.

Yarn
2 x 1¾ oz (50 g) balls—each approx 116 yds (106 m)— Katia Peru in shade 3 Off white (A)
Small amount of Sirdar Country Style DK in shade 417 Black (B)
Small piece of black felt
Black sewing thread

You will also need
Size US 9 (5.5 mm) knitting needles
Yarn sewing needle
Large-eyed embroidery needle
Standard sewing needle

Sizes
5-11 years (12 years and over)

Actual measurements
Approx 15½ in/39 cm (18 in/46 cm) circumference

Gauge (tension)
17 sts and 21 rows to 4 in (10 cm) square over stockinette (stocking) stitch using US 9 (5.5 mm) needles.

Main hat
(*make 1*)
Using US 9 (5.5 mm) needles and A, cast on 66(78) sts.
Row 1: [K2, p2] to last 2 sts, k2.
Row 2: [P2, k2] to last 2 sts, p2.
Rep Rows 1-2 once more.
Work 24(28) rows in st st beg with a k row.
Large size only:
Row 33: K5, [sl1, k2tog, psso, k10] 5 times, sl1, k2tog, psso, k5. (66 sts)
Row 34: P.
Both sizes:
Next row: K4, [sl1, k2tog, psso, k8] 5 times, sl1, k2tog, psso, k4. (54 sts)
Next and every WS row until stated otherwise: P.
Next RS row: K3, [sl1, k2tog, psso, k6] 5 times, sl1, k2tog, psso, k3. (42 sts)
Next RS row: K2, [sl1, k2tog, psso, k4] 5 times, sl1, k2tog, psso, k2. (30 sts)
Next RS row: K1, [sl1, k2tog, psso, k2] 5 times, sl1, k2tog, psso, k1. (18 sts)
Next row (WS): [P2tog] to end. (9 sts)
Break yarn leaving a long tail.
Thread yarn tail through rem sts, pull up tightly and secure.

Ears
(*make 2*)
Using US 9 (5.5 mm) needles and A, cast on 10 sts.
Work 6 rows in st st beg with a k row.
Row 7: K2tog, k6, ssk. (8 sts)
Row 8: P2tog, p4, p2tog. (6 sts)
Row 9: K2tog, k2, ssk. (4 sts)
Row 10: [P2tog] twice. (2 sts)
Row 11: [Inc1] twice. (4 sts)
Row 12: [Inc1 pwise, p1] twice. (6 sts)
Row 13: Inc1, k3, inc1, k1. (8 sts)
Row 14: Inc1 pwise, p5, inc1 pwise, p1. (10 sts)
Work 5 rows in st st beg with a k row.
Bind (cast) off on WS of work.

Making up and finishing
For general information on putting your hat together, see pages 104-107.

Join back seam of hat using the flat-seam technique (see page 104).

Fold ear pieces in half widthwise RS together so cast-on and bound- (cast-) off edges meet. Oversew around curved edges then turn ears RS out. Oversew lower edges. Stitch ears in place.

Cut two circles measuring 3/4 in (1.9 cm) in diameter in black felt for the eyes. Cut a rounded triangle measuring 1 1/2 in (3.8 cm) along its straight edge in black felt for the nose. Using B, secure eyes in place with a French knot (see page 106).

Using black sewing thread, oversew nose in place. Using B, work two straight stitches, one over the other, from bottom of nose to ribbed border of hat.

Chapter 4

useful information

tools & materials 94
stitches & techniques 95
yarn information 108
suppliers 110

tools & materials

The knitting needles, yarn, and other items that you need are listed at the beginning of each of the pattern instructions.

You can substitute the yarn with different brands, but you will need to be extra careful to check the gauge (tension). When using a different brand for the main part of the hat, it can affect the final look of your hat quite a lot. When calculating the quantity of yarn you require, it is the length of yarn in each ball that you need to check, rather than the weight. For details of the yarn used for these projects, see pages 108-109.

If substituting brands when the amount needed is very small—for example for the nose or the eyes—this will hardly affect the look of your hat at all, and it is very sensible to use up the yarns you have in your stash.

Sizes

Some of the projects in this book can be knitted in various sizes. In these cases, the instructions for larger sizes are given in round brackets after the main instructions. Once you have selected your size, it is important that you follow the information for that size only. Many knitters find it helpful to highlight the instructions for the size they are making before they begin knitting.

Gauge (tension)

To make sure that your hat is the right size, you will need to make sure that you are knitting to the same gauge (tension) as given in the instructions. The gauge is given as the number of stitches and rows you need to work to produce a 4-in (10-cm) square of knitting. If your square is smaller, you will need to reknit your gauge (tension) square using slightly larger needles and check it again. If your square is larger, you will need to reknit the square using slightly smaller needles and check it again.

Knitting with two strands at once

Quite a number of the patterns in this book involve knitting using two strands of double-knitting yarn at once. In most cases, this is quite easy to do by using the main yarn end, then pulling out the beginning of the ball of yarn from the center and knitting them together.

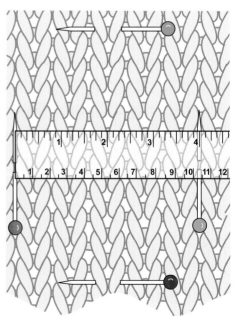

Gauge (tension)
Check your gauge using pins and a tape measure.

stitches & techniques

The two basic knitting stitches are the knit stitch and the purl stitch. By working a combination of these stitches, you can produce different knitted textures. These are the stitches and techniques used in the projects in this book.

Making a Slip Knot

You will need to make a slip knot to form your first cast-on stitch.

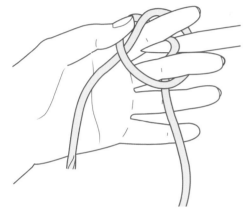

1. With the ball of yarn on your right, lay the end of the yarn on the palm of your left hand and hold it in place with your left thumb. With your right hand, take the yarn round your top two fingers to form a loop. Take the knitting needle through the back of the loop from right to left and use it to pick up the strand nearest to the yarn ball, as shown in the diagram. Pull the strand through to form a loop at the front.

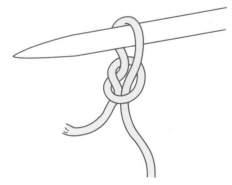

2. Slip the yarn off your fingers leaving the loop on the needle. Gently pull on both yarn ends to tighten the knot. Then pull on the yarn leading to the ball of yarn to tighten the knot on the needle.

Casting On

There are a few methods of casting on but the one used for the projects in this book is the cable method, which uses two needles.

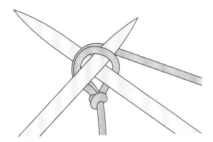

1. Make a slip knot as outlined above. Put the needle with the slip knot into your left hand. Insert the point of your other needle into the front of the slip knot and under the left needle. Wind the yarn from the ball of yarn around the tip of the right needle.

2. Using the tip of your needle, draw the yarn through the slip knot to form a loop. This loop is your new stitch. Slip the loop from the right needle onto the left needle.

3. To make the next stitch, insert the tip of your right needle between the two stitches. Wind the yarn over the right needle, from left to right, then draw the yarn through to form a loop. Transfer this loop to your left needle. Repeat until you have cast on the right number of stitches for your project.

Making a Knit Stitch

1. Hold the needle with the cast-on stitches in your left hand, and then insert the point of the right needle into the front of the first stitch from left to right. Wind the yarn around the point of the right needle, from left to right.

2. With the tip of your right needle, pull the yarn through the stitch to form a loop. This loop is your new stitch.

3. Slip the original stitch off the left needle by gently pulling your right needle to the right. Repeat these steps till you have knitted all the stitches on your left needle. To work the next row, transfer the needle with all the stitches into your left hand.

Making a Purl Stitch

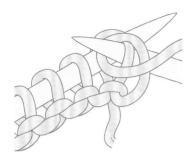

1. Hold the needle with the stitches in your left hand, and then insert the point of the right needle into the front of the first stitch from right to left. Wind the yarn around the point of the right needle, from right to left.

2. With the tip of the right needle, pull the yarn through the stitch to form a loop. This loop is your new stitch.

3. Slip the original stitch off the left needle by gently pulling your right needle to the right. Repeat these steps till you have purled all the stitches on your left needle. To work the next row, transfer the needle with all the stitches into your left hand.

Binding (Casting) Off

In most cases, you will bind (cast) off knitwise, which means you will knit the stitches before you bind (cast) them off.

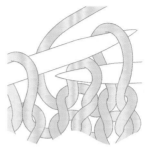

1. First knit two stitches in the normal way. With the point of your left needle, pick up the first stitch you have just knitted and lift it over the second stitch. Knit another stitch so that there are two stitches on your needle again. Repeat the process of lifting the first stitch over the second stitch. Continue this process until there is just one stitch remaining on the right needle.

2. Break the yarn, leaving a tail of yarn long enough to stitch your work together. Pull the tail all the way through the last stitch. Slip the stitch off the needle and pull it fairly tightly to make sure it is secure.

In a few of the projects in this book, you will need to bind (cast) off purlwise. This is exactly like ordinary binding (casting) off except that you purl the stitches rather than knit them.

Garter stitch

To make this stitch, you simply knit every row. This stitch is used for some of the hat borders and some of the earflaps.

Stockinette (stocking) stitch

To make this stitch, you work alternate rows of knit and purl stitches. The front of the fabric is the side when you work the knit rows. This stitch is used for the main part of the hats and other projects in this book.

Rib and Double rib

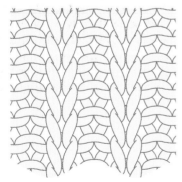

To make this stitch, you knit 1 stitch then purl 1 stitch across a row. On the next row, you knit the purl stitches and purl the knit stitches. Double rib is a variant in which you knit 2 stitches then purl 2 stitches. Like standard ribbing, it creates a slightly stretchy knitted fabric. Double rib is used on the borders of some of the hats and the cuffs and edges of other projects in this book.

Seed (moss) stitch

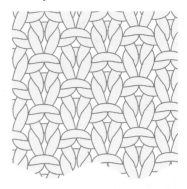

To make this stitch, knit and purl alternate stitches across a row. On the next row, knit the knit stitches and purl the purl stitches to create a firm, textured pattern. Seed (moss) stitch is used on the borders and earflaps of some of the hats in this book.

Extended garter stitch

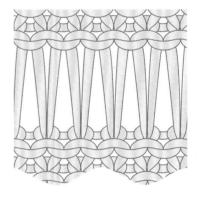

This is worked exactly like garter stitch except that you wind the yarn three times round the needle on the first row, instead of the normal once. On the second row, insert the needle through one part of the stitch only. When the "old" stitch drops off the needle as you work the stitch, it becomes elongated.

Abbreviations

These are the knitting abbreviations that you will need to know to follow the instructions in this book.

alt	alternate
beg	beginning
cont	continue
inc1	increase one stitch by knitting into the front then the back of the next stitch
K	knit
k2tog	knit the next 2 stitches together
kwise	by knitting the stitch or stitches
LH	left hand
MB	make one bobble (see page 31)
M1	make one stitch by picking up the horizontal loop before the next stitch and knitting into the back of it.
P	purl
p2tog	purl the next 2 stitches together
patt	pattern
pkso	pass knitted stitch over (the stitch just worked)
psso	pass slipped stitch over (the stitch just worked)
pwise	by purling the stitch or stitches
rep	repeat
rem	remaining
RH	right hand
RS	right side
sl1	slip one (slip a stitch onto the right-hand needle without knitting it)

ssk	slip, slip, knit (slip 2 stitches one at a time then knit the slipped stitches together)
st(s)	stitch(es)
st st	stocking stitch
WS	wrong side
cm	centimeter
g	gram
in	inch
mm	millimeter
m	meter(s)
oz	ounce
yd(s)	yard(s)
[]	Square brackets are used around instructions that you need to perform more than once. For example: [k2tog] 3 times means that you need to knit two stitches together three times.
()	When you have worked a row to increase or decrease the number of stitches on your needle, the number of stitches you should have after completing the row is given in round brackets at the end. For example: (6 sts) means that you should have six stitches on your needle. Round brackets also give the alternative stitch counts or row counts for different sizes. For example: K6(8) would mean you knit 6 stitches for the smaller size and 8 for the larger size.

Shaping up

You can shape your knitting pieces by increasing or decreasing the number of stitches on your needle. Each method results in a slightly different look.

Increasing

There are three main methods of increasing.

inc1

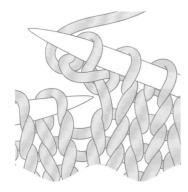

Start knitting your stitch in the normal way but instead of slipping the "old" stitch off the needle, knit into the back of it and then slip the "old" stitch off the needle in the normal way.

inc1 pwise

In a few of the patterns, you will also need to increase a stitch in this way on a purl row. This is done in the same way as increasing a stitch knitwise, except that you purl the stitches instead of knitting them.

M1

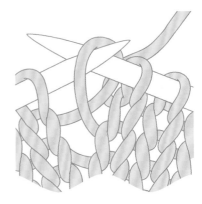

Pick up the horizontal strand between two stitches on your left-hand needle. Knit into the back of the loop and transfer the stitch to the right hand needle in the normal way. (It is important to knit into the back of the loop so that the yarn is twisted and does not form a hole in your work.)

Decreasing

There are several different ways of decreasing.

k2tog

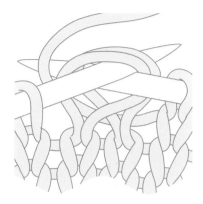

This is the simplest way of decreasing. Simply insert your needle through two stitches instead of the normal one when you begin your stitch and then knit them in the normal way.

p2tog

Simply insert your needle through two stitches instead of one when you begin your stitch and then purl them in the normal way.

ssk

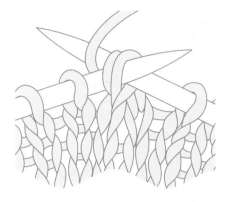

This is another way of decreasing. Slip one stitch and then the next stitch on to your right-hand needle, without knitting them. Then insert the left-hand needle from left to right through the front loops of both the slipped stitches and knit them as normal.

sl1, k2tog, psso

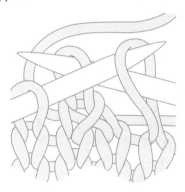

This is a way of decreasing two stitches at a time and is used in most of the hat patterns in this book. Slip the first stitch from the left to the right needle without knitting it. Knit the next two stitches together as described above left. Then lift the slipped stitch over the stitch in front.

Other techniques

Here are a few other techniques that are used in some of the projects.

Making a bobble

Bobbles are made by working a number of increases into one stitch and then decreasing. Bobbles are used in just one pattern in this book (the hedgehog hat on page 31). They are worked in the following way:

K1, P1, K1 all into the next stitch, which is the place where the bobble will be.
Turn work and P3.
Turn work again and slip 1, k2tog, psso.
Continue along the row until you get to the stitch where you need to work the next bobble.

On some bobbles you will also need to decrease the number of stitches while you are working your bobble. This is done in the following way:

K2tog then P1, K1 into the same stitch.
Turn work and P3.
Turn work again and slip, k2tog, psso.

Picking up stitches along an edge

For some projects, you will need to pick up stitches along either a horizontal edge (usually the cast-on edge of your knitting) or a vertical edge (the edges of your rows of knitting).

Along a vertical edge

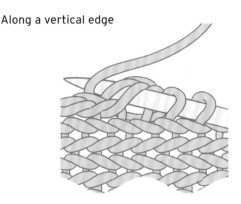

This instruction is written as "pick up and k" as it involves picking up stitches and knitting them as you go along.

With the right side of your knitting facing you, insert your needle from the front to back between the first and second stitches of the first row. Wind you yarn around the needle and pull through a loop to form the new stitch. Normally you have more gaps between rows than stitches you need to pick up and knit. To make sure your work is even, you will have to miss a gap every few rows.

Along a horizontal edge

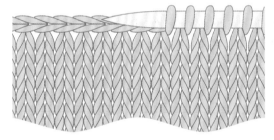

This is worked in the same way as picking up stitches along a vertical edge except that you will work through the cast-on stitches rather than the gaps between rows. You will normally have the same number of stitches to pick up and knit as there are gaps between rows.

Knitting in different colors

If you are knitting in stripes, you can simply join your second color at one end. If the stripes are narrow, you do not need to break and rejoin your yarn between stripes.

Stranding

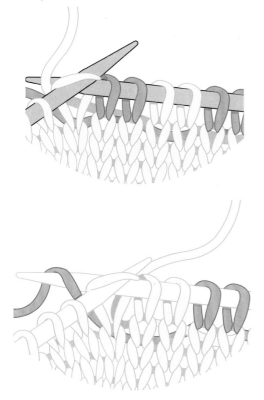

If you are knitting just a few stitches in a different color, you can simply leave the color you are not using on the wrong side of your work and pick it up again when you need to.

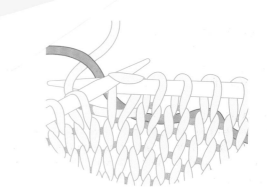

If you are knitting more than a few stitches in a different color, but only for a few rows, you can weave the yarns into the back of your stitches as you work.

On a knit row, insert your right-hand needle into the next stitch and lay the yarn you want to weave in over the needle. Knit the stitch, taking it under the yarn you are weaving in, making sure to pull through only the main yarn. Repeat this every few stitches until you need to use the second yarn again.

On a purl row, use the same method to work in the yarn.

Color change (intarsia)

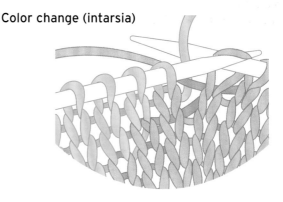

If you are knitting blocks of different colors within your project, which you will need to do for quite a few of the hats in this book, you will need to use a technique called intarsia. This involves using separate balls of yarn for each area and twisting the yarns together where they join to avoid creating a gap.

On the right side
When you want to change colors and the color change is vertical or sloping out to the right, take the first color over the second color. Then pick up the second color, so the strands of yarn cross each other.

On the wrong side
This is worked in almost the same way as on the right side. When you want to change colors and the color change is vertical or sloping out to the left, take the first color over the second color. Then pick up the second color, so the strands of yarn cross each other.

Putting it all together

How you piece your work together can make all the difference to the final look of your project, so it is worth taking your time. Here are few useful techniques and tips.

Flat seam

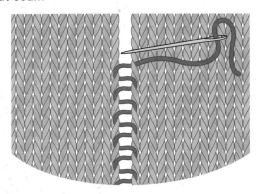

This is the technique used for sewing the back seams of the hats. Unlike mattress stitch, it creates a join that is completely flat.

Lay the two edges to be joined side by side with the right side facing you. Pick up the very outermost strand of knitting from one side and then the other, working your way along the seam and pulling your yarn up firmly every few stitches.

Mattress stitch

There are two versions of this stitch - one used to join two vertical edges (such as the seams on the Zebra Wrist Warmers and Tiger Boot Toppers) and the other used to join two horizontal edges (such as the top edge of the rabbit hat).

Vertical edges

Place the two edges side by side with the right side facing you. Take your needle under the running thread between the first two stitches of one side then under the corresponding running thread of the other side. Pull your yarn up fairly firmly every few stitches.

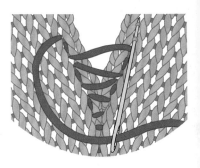

Horizontal edges

Place the two edges side by side with the right side facing you. Take your needle under the two "legs" of the last row of stitches on the first piece of knitting. Then take your needle under the two "legs" of the corresponding stitch on the second piece of knitting. Pull your yarn up fairly firmly every few stitches.

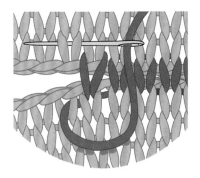

Ankle Warmers
This chart is for the project on page 87.

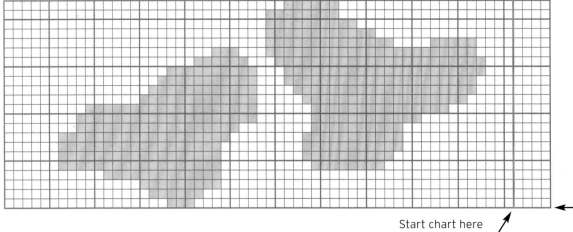

Start chart here for smaller size

Start chart here for larger size

Oversewing

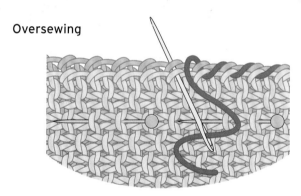

This stitch is used to seam small pieces of work (such as some of the animal ears). It is normally worked with the right sides of your work together.

Take the yarn from the front of your work, over the edge of the seam and out through the front again a short distance further on.

Sewing on the noses and eye pieces

Flat pieces, such as the noses and eyes, can be simply oversewn in place. Stretch the piece very slightly as you work to make sure that it lies flat.

Sewing on the ears, horns and antlers

These can be either oversewn in place or fastened using a technique similar to mattress stitch. Fasten the ears along both the front and back edges to make sure they are secure. The horns and antlers should be fastened so that the base forms a circular shape where it meets the main part of the hat to make sure they stay upright.

Concealing yarn tails

When your knitting is complete, you will have a few ends of yarn that need concealing. The easiest way to do this is to run a few small stitches forwards then backwards through your work, ideally in a seam. It is a good idea to use your embroidery needle to do this and take the tail between the strands that make up your yarn, as this will help make sure the tail stays in place.

Dunking and drying

Sometimes when you have finished your knitting, the shape may not be quite as even as you would like. If this is the case, soak your item thoroughly (but do not leave it to soak), reshape it, then place it flat and leave it to dry naturally.

Embroidery techniques

Some of the animals' features are embroidered using double knitting (DK) yarn. These include some of the eyes and noses and some of the markings. When embroidering on knitting, take your needle in and out of your work between the strands that make up your yarn rather than between the stitches themselves. This will help make your embroidery look more even.

Chain stitch

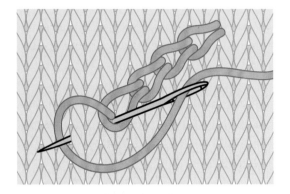

Bring your yarn out at the starting point on the front of your work. Take your needle back into your knitting just next to your starting point, leaving a loop of yarn. Bring your needle out of your work again, a stitch length further on and catch in the loop. Pull your thread up firmly, but not so tight that it pulls your knitting. Continue in this way till the line, coil, or circle is complete.

Stem stitch

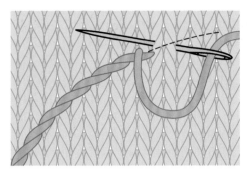

Take your yarn out at your starting point at the front of your work, then down into your work a little way along. Take the yarn out again, about midway between the other two points. Repeat this process until you have completed the line, remembering to keep your yarn on the same side of your needle as you work.

Straight stitch

To make this stitch, simply take your yarn out at your starting point and back down into your work where you want the stitch to end.

French knots

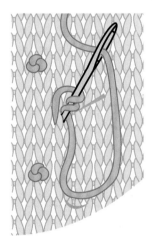

Bring your yarn out at your starting point, where you want the French knot to sit. Wind the yarn around the needle the required number of times, then take it back into your work, just to the side of your starting point. Then take your needle out at the point for the next French knot or, if you are working the last or a single knot, to the back of your work. Continue pulling your needle through your work and slide the knot off the needle and onto your knitting.

Crochet techniques

While the projects in this book are all knitted rather than crocheted, for some hats you will need to know how to work a crochet chain or how to work a crochet edging.

Make a crochet chain

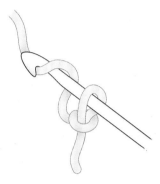

1. Make a slip knot on the crochet hook in the same way as if you were starting to cast on some knitting. Holding the slip stitch on the hook, wind the yarn around the hook from the back to the front, then catch the yarn in the crochet-hook tip.

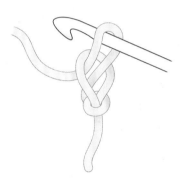

2. Pull the yarn through the slip stitch on your crochet hook to make the second link in the chain.

3. Continue in this way till the chain is the length that you need.

Work a crochet edging

A crochet edging can be worked along a horizontal edge or a vertical edge, but the basic technique is the same.

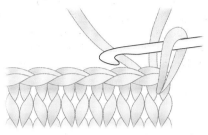

1. Insert your crochet hook in the first space between stitches. Wind the yarn round the hook and pull a loop of yarn through.

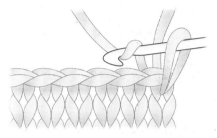

2. Wind the yarn round your hook again and then pull the loop through to make a single chain.

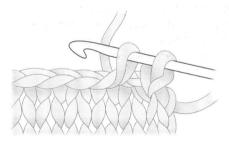

3. Insert your hook through the next stitch, wind the yarn round the hook, and pull through a second loop of yarn.

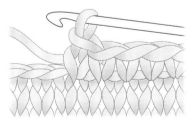

4. Wind the yarn round your hook and pull a loop of yarn through both loops on the hook. Repeat steps 3 and 4, inserting the hook into the spaces between stitches in an even pattern.

For crochet edging along a vertical edge, insert your hook into the spaces between the edges of your rows rather than the spaces between stitches.

yarn information

These are the yarns used in this book. For information on substituting yarns, see Tools and Materials on page 94.

Yarn	Composition	Length and weight
Debbie Bliss Angel	76% super kid mohair, 24% silk	219 yds (200 m) in a 1 oz (25 g) ball
Debbie Bliss Cashmerino DK	55% wool, 33% acrylic, 12% cashmere	120 yds (110 m) in a 1¾ oz (50 g) ball
Debbie Bliss Rialto DK	100% merino wool	115 yds (105 m) in a 1¾ oz (50 g) ball
Katia Maxi Merino	55% merino wool, 45% acrylic	137 yds (125 m) in a 1¾ oz (50 g) ball
Katia Merino Blend	55% merino wool, 45% acrylic	262 yds (240 m) in a 3½ oz (100 g) ball
Katia Peru	40% wool, 40% acrylic, 20% alpaca	116 yds (106 m) in a 3½ oz (50 g) ball
King Cole Merino Blend DK	100% wool	122 yds (112 m) in a 3½ oz (50 g) ball
Patons Diploma Gold DK	55% wool, 25% acrylic, 20% nylon	131 yds (120 m) in a 1¾ oz (50 g) ball
Patons Fairytale Dreamtime DK	100% wool	98 yds (90 m) in a 1¾ oz (50 g) ball
Rowan Amy Butler Belle Organic DK	50% wool, 50% cotton	131 yds (120 m) in a 1¾ oz (50 g) ball
Rowan Big Wool	100% merino wool	87 yds (80 m) in a 3½ oz (100 g) ball
Rowan Cashsoft DK	57% extra fine merino wool, 33% acrylic microfiber, 10% cashmere	126 yds (115 m) in a 1¾ oz (50 g) ball
Rowan Creative Focus Worsted	75% wool, 25% alpaca	219 yds (200 m) in a 3½ oz (100 g) ball

Yarn	Composition	Length and weight
Rowan Felted Tweed DK	50% merino wool, 25% alpaca, 25% viscose	191 yds (175 m) in a 1¾ oz (50 g) ball
Rowan Pure Wool DK	100% wool	136 yds (125 m) in a 1¾ oz (50 g) ball
Rowan Wool Cotton DK	50% wool, 50% cotton	123 yds (113 m)) in a 1¾ oz (50 g) ball
Sirdar Big Softie	51% wool, 49% acrylic	49 yds (45 m) in a 1¾ oz (50 g) ball
Sirdar Click Chunky	70% acrylic, 30% wool	81 yds (75 m) in a 1¾ oz (50 g) ball
Sirdar Click DK	70% acrylic, 30% wool	164 yds (150 m) in a 1¾ oz (50 g) ball
Sirdar Connemara Tweed Effect Chunky	51% wool, 49% acrylic	81 yds (75 m) in a 1¾ oz (50 g) ball
Sirdar Country Style DK	40% nylon, 30% wool, 30% acrylic	109 yds (100 m) in a 1¾ oz (50 g) ball
Sublime extra fine merino DK	100% extra fine merino wool	127 yds (116 m) in a 1¾ oz (50 g) ball
Twilleys Freedom Purity Chunky	85% wool, 15% alpaca	79 yds (72 m) in a 1¾ oz (50 g) ball
Wendy Merino DK	100% merino wool	127 yds (116 m) in a 1¾ oz (50 g) ball
Wendy Norse Chunky	50% wool, 50% acrylic	87 yds (80 m) in a 1¾ oz (50 g) ball
Wendy Osprey	20% alpaca, 20% wool, 30% polyamide, 30% acrylic	109 yds (100 m) in a 1¾ oz (50 g) ball

suppliers

UK

Debbie Bliss Yarns
Designer Yarns Ltd
Units 8-10 Newbridge Industrial
Estate
Pitt Street, Keighly
West Yorkshire BD21 4PQ
Tel: +44 (0) 1535 664222
www.debbieblissonline.com

Katia Yarns
Barcelona, Spain
Tel: +34 93 828 38 19
www.katia.com
Website gives details of local
UK suppliers

King Cole
King Cole Ltd
Merrie Mills
Elliot Street, Silsden
West Yorkshire BD20 0DE
Tel: +44 (0) 1535 650230
www.kingcole.co.uk

Patons
Coats Crafts UK
Green Lane Mill
Holmfirth
West Yorkshire HD9 2DX
Tel +44 (0) 1484 681881
www.coatscrafts.co.uk

Rowan
Rowan Yarns
Green Lane Mill
Holmfirth
West Yorkshire HD9 2DX
Tel: +44 (0) 1484 681881
www.knitrowan.com

Sirdar
Sirdar Spinning Ltd
Flanshaw Lane
Wakefield
West Yorkshire WF2 9ND
Tel: +44 (0) 1924 231682
www.sirdar.co.uk

Deramores
Online store only
Tel: 0845 519 457
www.deramores.com
Patons, Sublime, Twilleys, Wendy

Mavis Crafts
Online and retail store
Tel: +44 (0) 208 950 5445
www.mavis-crafts.com
Katia, Sirdar, Sublime, Wendy

John Lewis
Retail stores and online
www.johnlewis.com
Telephone numbers of local
stores on website
Tel: 08456 049 049
(Customer Services)

USA

Knitting Fever Inc.
PO Box 336
315 Bayview Avenue
Amityville
NY 11701
Tel: +1 516 546 3600
www.knittingfever.com
Debbie Bliss, Katia, Sirdar, Sublime

Westminster Fibers
165 Ledge Street
Nashua
NH 03060
Tel: +800 445 9276
www.westmnsterfibers.com
Rowan

Canada

Diamond Yarn
155 Martin Ross Unit 3
Toronto, ON
M3J 2L9
Tel: +1 416 736 6111
www.diamondyarn.com
Debbie Bliss, Katia, Sirdar, Sublime

Patons
320 Livingstone Avenue South
Box 40
Listowel, ON
N4W 3H3
Tel: +1 888 368 8401
www.patonsyarns.com

Westminster Fibers
10 Roybridge Gate Suite 200
Vaughn, ON
L4H 3MB
Tel: +800 445 9276
www.westmnsterfibers.com
Rowan

Australia

Prestige Yarns Pty Ltd
PO Box 39
Bulli
NSW 2516
Tel: +61 (0)2 4285 6669
www.prestigeyarns.com
Debbie Bliss

Texyarns International PTY Ltd
105-115 Dover Street
Cremorne, Melbourne
VIC 3121
Tel: +61 (0)3 9427 9009
www.texyarns.com
Katia

Yarn Over
Shop 1 265 Baker Street
Keperra,
QLD 4054
Tel: +61 (0)7 3851 2608
Patons

Rowan
www.knitrowan.com
Online store locator

Creative Images
PO Box 106
Hastings
VIC 3915
Tel: +61 (0)3 5979 1555
Sirdar

index

abbreviations 99
ankle warmers, cow 87
antlers, sewing on 105

babies
  bee hat 20-1
  chick hat 10-11
  ladybug hat 12-14
  rabbit bonnet 16-17
  robin hat 18-19
balaclava, dragon 65-7
bear, hat/mittens 42-5
bee, hat/bootees 20-3
binding off 97
blocks, knitting 103
bobble, making 102
boot toppers, tiger 80
bootees
  bee 22-3
  ladybug 15

casting on/off 96, 97
cat, hat/mittens 74-7
chain stitch 106
chick hat 10-11
children
  bear hat 42-4
  dragon balaclava 65-7
  fish hat 52-3
  fox hat 58-61
  frog hat 29-30
  hedgehog hat 31-3
  lion hat 54-7
  monkey hat 50-1
  monster hat 38-9
  mouse hat 40-1
  octopus hat 46-7
  owl hat 26-8
  panda hat 68-9
  penguin hat 48-9
  reindeer hat 62-4
  zebra hat 34-6
colors, knitting in different
  103
cow, hat/ankle warmers
  84-7
crochet techniques 107

decreasing 101
dogs, hound hat 81-3

dragon balaclava 65-7

earflaps, positioning 27
ears, sewing on 105
edging
  crochet 107
  picking up stitches 102
embroidery stitches 106
eyes, sewing on 105

fish hat 52-3
flat seam 104
fox hat 58-61
French knots 106
frog hat 29-30

garter stitch 98
gauge square 6, 94

hedgehog hat 31-3
horns, sewing on 105
hound hat 81-3

increasing 100
intarsia 103

knit stitch 96
koala hat 72-3

ladybug/ladybird,
  hat/bootees 12-15
lion hat 54-7

making up 104-7
materials 94
mattress stitch 104
mittens/wrist warmers
  bear 45
  cat 77
  zebra 37
monkey hat 50-1
monster hat 38-9
moss stitch 98
mouse hat 40-1

noses, sewing on 105

octopus hat 46-7
oversewing 105
owl hat 26-8

panda hat 68-9
penguin hat 48-9
pig hat 88-9
polar bear hat 90-1
purl stitch 97

rabbit bonnet 16-17
reindeer hat 62-4
rib 98
robin hat 18-19

seams 104-5
seed stitch 98
shaping
  completed items 105
  increase/decrease 100-1
sizes 6, 94
skill level 6
slip knot 95
stem stitch 106
stitches
  crochet 107
  embroidery 106
  knitting 95-8
  picking up 102
stockinette/stocking stitch
  98
straight stitch 106
stranding yarns 103
stripes, color change 103

techniques 95-7
tension square 6, 94
tiger, hat/boot toppers
  78-80
tools 94

washing 105
weaving in yarns 103
wrist warmers, zebra 37

yarn
  color change 103
  information 108-9
  sewing in ends 105
  substituting 94
  suppliers 110
  using two strands 94
young at heart
  cat hat/mittens 74-7
  cow hat/ankle warmers
    84-7
  hound hat 81-3
  koala hat 72-3
  pig hat 88-9
  polar bear hat 90-1
  tiger hat/boot toppers
    78-80

zebra, hat/wrist warmers
  34-7

acknowledgments

I would like to thank the team at Cico for having the idea for this book, for asking me to do it, and for putting it together so beautifully. Thanks as well to Pam and Mick Conquest at Mavis of Bushey, my local wool shop, for their help with the yarns. I would also like to express my appreciation and admiration for Tricia McKenzie, my eagle-eyed pattern checker. A big thanks as well to my sister Louise Turner for her help in knitting the projects and to my aunt Sheelagh Magee for teaching me to knit in the first place, all those years ago. Thanks as well to the gorgeous models who have shown off my projects so well. Finally, thank you to my partner Roger and son Louis for their patience—and for living in a house full of knitting yarns.